Simple Ways to Break
the Rules and Discover
Your Hidden Genius

How to
Think Like
Einstein

*Simple Ways to Break
the Rules and Discover
Your Hidden Genius*

How to
Think Like
Einstein

BY SCOTT THORPE

SOURCEBOOKS, INC.®
NAPERVILLE, ILLINOIS

This publication is designed to provide accurate and authoritative information in regard to the subject matter covered. It is sold with the understanding that the publisher is not engaged in rendering legal, accounting, or other professional service. If legal advice or other expert assistance is required, the services of a competent professional person should be sought.—*From a Declaration of Principles Jointly Adopted by a Committee of theAmerican Bar Association and a Committee of Publishers and Associations*

All brand names and product names used in this book are trademarks, registered trademarks, or trade names of their respective holders. Sourcebooks, Inc., is not associated with any product or vendor in this book.

Published by Sourcebooks, Inc.
P.O. Box 4410, Naperville, Illinois 60567-4410
(630) 961-3900
FAX: (630) 961-2168

Library of Congress Cataloging-in-Publication Data

Thorpe, Scott.
   How to think like Einstein: simple ways to break the rules and discover your
   hidden genius/Scott Thorpe.
     p. cm.
   Includes index.
   ISBN 1-57071-585-8 (alk. paper)
     1. Problem solving. 2. Creative thinking. I. Title.

BF449 .T48 2000
153.4—dc21

                                                              00-044044

Printed and bound in the United States of America
VHG 10 9 8 7 6 5 4 3 2 1

To Dr. Alder for getting me started and
to Vicki for letting me finish.

Many thanks to Hillel Black for his skillful
editing and insightful suggestions.

TABLE OF CONTENTS

CHAPTER ONE

Einstein's Secret

"Common sense is
the collection of
prejudices acquired
by age eighteen."

—ALBERT EINSTEIN

This book will teach you to create solutions to your toughest, even impossible, problems. You will learn the techniques implicit in the solutions of history's greatest problem solver, Albert Einstein. Einstein solved some of the world's most bewildering problems. He was successful because he had a very different way of thinking. You can learn to think in the same way by using his techniques.

These techniques, and those of others presented here, are not just for unraveling the mysteries of the universe. By learning new ways to solve problems, you can increase the profitability of your business, improve educational opportunities for your children, make artistic and creative breakthroughs, and enhance the quality of your life. Tough problems of all kinds can be resolved because one universal principle is at the core of learning to think like a genius: **you've got to break the rules.**

Einstein was one of the world's most natural rule breakers, the "James Dean" of science. It wasn't just physical laws that he challenged. He flaunted tradition and outraged governments. Breaking rules caused him constant trouble, but Einstein's audacious willingness to fracture any rule was at the core of his genius. Einstein was a great problem solver because he was a superb rule breaker. It is a common trait of genius, and a skill that can be learned and cultivated. We can all think like Einstein, if we just learn to break the rules.

Rule Ruts

"Few people are capable of expressing with equanimity opinions which differ from the prejudices of their social environment. Most people are even incapable of forming such opinions."

—Albert Einstein

If you can't solve a problem, it is probably because you are stuck in a rule rut. We all have rules—ingrained patterns of thinking that we mistake for truth. Our rules form naturally. Ideas become rules with repeated use. When a rule rut forms, all conflicting ideas are ignored.

Rules are not always bad things. They are like railroad tracks. If you want to go where the track goes, they are perfect. But like destinations without a rail line, some solutions cannot be reached with our rules. The only way to get there is to leave the tracks.

Rules stunt innovative thinking because they seem so right. They hide the numerous superior solutions that exist, but are outside our rule ruts. These great solutions will only be found by breaking the rules.

No one is immune to rule ruts. Even Einstein was stymied for years by one of his prejudices. But to him, the offending rule seemed inviolable.

You may not be interested in discovering the laws that govern the universe, but you still have tough problems to solve. Your problems may even be tougher than Einstein's. You may be competing against smart people in an environment that changes every time you figure it out. Your challenge may seem impossible. But there is an answer—if you can learn to break the rules.

The real obstacle when we are faced with an impossible problem is inside us. It is our experiences, mistaken assumptions, half-truths, misplaced generalities, and habits that keep us from brilliant solutions. The great new ideas, the vital solutions exist. They are just outside of the prevailing thought. Otherwise someone would have found them already. You must break the rules to solve impossible problems.

BREAKING RULES AND SOLVING PROBLEMS

"I sometimes ask myself how it came about that I was the one to develop the theory of relativity. The reason, I think, is that a normal adult never stops to think about problems of space and time. These are things which he has thought about as a child. But my intellectual development was retarded, as a result of which I began to wonder about space and time only when I had already grown up."

—ALBERT EINSTEIN

Saying that rule breaking was the secret to Einstein's genius is a big claim. He was also naturally brilliant and extremely tenacious. How do we know that rule breaking wasn't just an ancillary quirk of genius? Let's do a simple thought experiment to learn what was responsible for Einstein's great ideas. Einstein loved thought experiments, so it is appropriate that he is the subject of ours. We will examine Einstein's intelligence, knowledge, and rule breaking, and see how they affected his creative output. And, we will do it without any complicated physics or math.

Einstein's intelligence was consistently high throughout his life. We will represent this as a horizontal line in our thought experiment (Figure 1.1). Einstein's vast knowledge of mathematics and science increased steadily throughout his life. We will represent his knowledge as a line sloping upward. So far this is just what we would expect from a genius.

But when we look at Einstein's problem-solving output, something seems wrong. Beginning in 1905, just out of the university, Einstein had a prolonged period of truly revolutionary thinking. For almost twenty years, he made important advances in science. The most profound

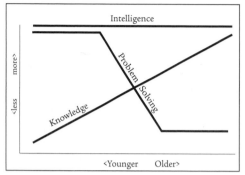

Figure 1.1: A Thought Experiment

breakthroughs came during a remarkable year at the beginning of his career. But, in later years, Einstein's problem solving dropped off. We will represent this decline as a downward sloping line. Einstein continued to work hard on the important problems of physics. He was still brilliant. He knew even more about physics and math. He had uninterrupted time for his work and collaboration with the world's greatest minds. But he didn't solve any more important scientific problems.

We would expect Einstein's problem solving to correlate with his intelligence and knowledge. Instead, his problem-solving ability declined as his knowledge increased. Innovation was highest when knowledge was lowest. It seems wrong. We would dismiss the results of our thought experiment if the pattern weren't repeated in the lives of so many brilliant people. People willing to break the rules solve impossible problems. They are usually newcomers to the field, without the baggage of years of precedent.

It wasn't Einstein the wise old professor that first solved the mysteries of space and time. He was a kid just out of college. He worked at the Swiss patent office reviewing improvements to laundry wringers. He did physics on the side. And he was breaking rules.

The problem Einstein solved that gave us $E = mc^2$ was an old one. A generation of scientists had been trying to understand why light always seems to be going the same speed relative to the observer. Regardless of whether you are moving toward a beam of light or away from it, the light's speed is the same. It was one of science's most important and baffling problems. Many brilliant people came close to a solution, but they all failed because of a rule.

Hundreds of years earlier, Isaac Newton had decreed that time was absolute. It did not run faster or slower. It was the universe's constant. Newton's reasoning made sense, and the idea became firmly and deeply embedded in the mind of every scientist that followed. It was at the foundation of all scientific knowledge. Scientists couldn't even imagine breaking the "time is absolute" rule, so they couldn't solve the problem.

Einstein had no trouble violating Newton's "time is absolute" rule. He simply imagined that time could run faster for one object than for another. That changed the problem completely. A few lines of math (which can be found in Appendix B) started Einstein down a road that has revolutionized our world. Einstein solved science's most difficult problem by breaking a rule.

If rule breaking was the secret to Einstein's genius, then we should expect his problem solving to decline when he didn't break the rules—and that is exactly what happened. As physicists built on Einstein's work, they created a new theory. At its core was the concept of uncertainty—that some outcomes couldn't be predicted. Einstein found uncertainty troubling. Reason told him that the universe must be predictable. He hated uncertainty. He couldn't believe that God would play dice with the universe. His discoveries stopped. He was another smart man confused by his own common sense.

IMPOSSIBLE PROBLEMS: WINNING AT TIC-TAC-TOE

Most impossible problems are like winning at tic-tac-toe. Winning seems impossible. You may play over and over, using different strategies, without any success. But you can win at tic-tac-toe and solve other hopeless problems, if you break the rules.

Extra Turns

It is easy to win at tic-tac-toe if you take an extra turn. "What?" you are probably thinking. "You can't do that!" OK, it is cheating, but it works. It solves the problem. The choice is break the rules or fail.

You might not want to cheat at tic-tac-toe, but what about an important problem, a tough problem that you need solved? Could you break the rules to create a solution? Of course, I am not talking about moral

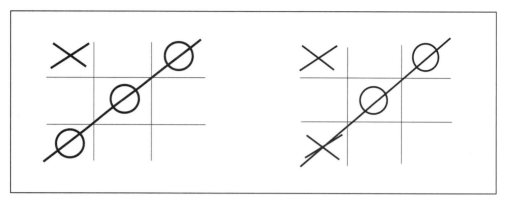

Figure 1.2: Extra Turns   **Figure 1.3: Use the Other Guy's Asset**

laws, but rather the rules in your head that dictate how the problem should be solved.

Few people consider taking an extra turn (cheating) in the real world, but it is actually a time-honored solution. For example, after a battle during the American Civil War, Robert E. Lee told his subordinates that he was positive that General Grant would move to Spotsylvania, since that was his best option. Lee devised a short cut to that position and told his troops to move by it. Lee's troops took an extra turn, in a manner of speaking, and marched to Spotsylvania before Grant's army could arrive.

Extra turns are common in business as well. When the makers of Tylenol learned that Datril, a similar pain reliever, would be launched at a significant discount, they took an extra turn. They matched Datril's price before Datril could advertise its cost advantage. The Datril introduction fizzled and Tylenol maintained its market share.

Use the Other Guy's Asset

There are many ways to win at tic-tac-toe, or solve impossible problems. It isn't hard to get three in a row, if you use an *X* with two of your *O*s. Why limit yourself to your own ideas?

Admiral Harry Yarnell of the United States Navy originally developed the basic plan for Japan's attack on Pearl Harbor. He determined the best

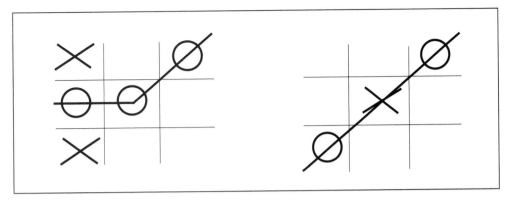

Figure 1.4: Define Victory Flexibly   **Figure 1.5: Cooperate**

routes and described the strategy. He even demonstrated how it should work with two U.S. aircraft carriers in 1932. The Imperial Japanese Navy, recognizing the value of the idea, turned an American admiral's plan into their own successful attack against the United States Navy. It didn't bother them to use American battle plans. If it works, use it, regardless of the source. Whose idea could you use to solve your problem?

Define Victory Flexibly

You can win at tic-tac-toe, or solve other tough problems, if you use a flexible definition of victory. Allow for a kink in your row and you will win every time. Sometimes our conditions for victory are too stringent or inappropriate. When Winston Churchill was thirty-five and served as the home secretary, some of his friends were discussing how they had not expected to rise to their important positions so early in life. But Churchill just fumed, "Napoleon won Austerlitz at my age." Churchill couldn't win his personal contest with ambition because his definition of victory was too lofty. Changing the definition of success can make a solution possible.

Cooperate

The rule that someone must lose may be your biggest obstacle to either of you winning. Cooperate with your opponent so that you both win. I once watched a building burn to the ground. The owner was happy about it. So was the fire department. The owner needed his building demolished, and the fire department needed a place to practice their fire fighting. Both needs were solved with perfect synergy.

All of these solutions break the rules of tic-tac-toe, just as Einstein broke the rules of physics. You will not win at tic-tac-toe or solve impossible problems just by trying harder. You must break the rules.

EINSTEIN THINKING: BREAKING THE RULES

"Man tries to make for himself in the fashion that suits him best a simplified and intelligent picture of the world; he then tries to substitute this cosmos of his for the world of experience, and thus overcome it."

—ALBERT EINSTEIN

Thinking like Einstein works because the biggest obstacles to solving tough problems are in our heads. Breaking rules is hard. This is why there are so many smart people but so few Einsteins. You may have to violate a cherished rule to solve your toughest problem. Henry Ford made a fortune mass-producing identical, practical Model T cars. He almost lost that fortune because of his Model T rule. His competitors offered frills and options for the increasingly affluent middle class. Henry lost market shares making black Model T cars because he wouldn't break his own rule.

The rule you need to break may transgress common sense. You and your colleagues will be certain you are making a foolish mistake. But violating common sense may be the only way to solve the problem. By his own admission, Einstein's greatest mistake was modifying some equations to make the universe conform to his common sense. His calculations told him that the universe must either be expanding or contracting. But he felt that it must be static—one glance at the night sky confirmed this truth. Only later, when astronomers observed the expansion of the universe, did he correct his theory.

You can solve your own impossible problems like Einstein. It won't be easy to do, but it will be fun when you do it. Breaking rules is exhilarating. If you can learn to break the rules that are holding you back, the universe is yours.

CHAPTER TWO

Thinking Like Einstein

> "There is nothing that is a more certain sign of insanity than to do the same thing over and over and expect the results to be different."
>
> ALBERT EINSTEIN

YOU CAN THINK LIKE EINSTEIN

You can think in the same imaginative, precedent-breaking way that Einstein thought. Rule breaking is our birthright. We are a race of innovators. Slow, soft humans are the last creatures one would expect to survive in a jungle of a world. But we beat the sharper claws because we can break the rules, changing strategies in seconds, not generations.

Children start as superb innovators. They spin fanciful solutions undeterred by any obstacles. Even as we grow older, we admire bold thinking. Revolution is chic. Trendsetters are idolized. It is demeaning to be called unoriginal, staid, or conventional. We relish opportunities to break the rules.

But if change, innovation, and creation are such powerful human traits, why do we still get stuck in rule ruts? What happens to our wonderful natural ability to break the rules?

Trained to Obey the Rules

"The only thing that interferes with my learning is my education."

—ALBERT EINSTEIN

Our talent for breaking rules atrophies because we are trained to obey the rules. Education, socialization, and standardization work together to make staying in our rule ruts habitual.

Einstein was never a conformist. We remember the quiet professor, but the Einstein who gave us relativity had an attitude problem. He rarely attended classes, preferring to spend his time in the laboratory. It was a difficult education and Einstein suffered much for his independence. His professors withheld the recommendation that would have allowed him to secure a university position. But Einstein acquired the knowledge of his day without becoming its slavish acolyte. It was a tremendous advantage.

Once out of school, we continue to learn to follow procedure, go with the crowd, and respect authority. Even organizations that need innovation discourage new thinking. If someone makes a "crazy" suggestion in a meeting, no one says, "Wow, that kind of original thinking may lead to a novel solution." Instead, they roll their eyes and return to the discussion. We have been taught to learn the rules, use the rules, and revere the rules.

Einstein did much of his best thinking when he was completely isolated from the rest of the scientific community. While he worked at the patent office, no one directed his physics research. There was no tenure committee to intimidate him. No department head reigned in his wild ideas. He didn't attend conventions to learn what everyone else was thinking. Einstein was free to create great solutions. And he did.

Precedent has a powerful influence on our thinking. For example, the most modern, state-of-the-art train still runs on a standard gauge, or track width. The gauge became standard on American railroads because British engineers, who had used the same gauge on their railroads, built them. British railroads originally adopted the standard because the carriage tooling was available to make axles that size. All carriages used that dimension of axle to fit in the ruts of British roads. British roads started as Roman roads. Roman chariots originally made the ruts. The axles of Roman chariots were built to accommodate two Roman horses.

A modern transportation system cannot escape what was perfect for Roman horses, just as your thoughts are still shaped by generations of old thinking. We continue down millennia-old ruts without recognizing that the reason for the rule has disappeared. Even worse, we become experts.

We Become Experts

"To punish me for my contempt for authority, fate made me an authority myself."

—ALBERT EINSTEIN

It is not unusual that Einstein the great rule breaker was also Einstein the novice. Novices conceive the breakthroughs that win Nobel prizes. They receive the awards and recognition when they are famous experts, but the ideas were created as novices.

Novices are the best rule breakers. It is easier to break a rule that one has just learned. Novices know the concepts, but can still ignore them. It is like learning the customs of another culture. An outsider can learn a new custom and follow it, but he can also violate it without anxiety because the rule is not ingrained. A native, on the other hand, would not even consider the violation because the rule rut is too deep.

We all develop expertise in one field or another. As we do, our novice's talent for breaking rules fades. Ideas become inviolable rules. We would no more break our rules than defy gravity.

EVERYONE CAN THINK LIKE EINSTEIN

"The whole of science is nothing more than the refinement of everyday thinking."

—ALBERT EINSTEIN

Thinking like Einstein is something that everyone can do, regardless of age or education. Even experts can be outstanding innovators. Alexander

Graham Bell's career as a teacher of the deaf gave him great insight into speech when he started work on the telephone. He had one other advantage—he knew little about electric devices. While everyone else focused on improving telegraphs, Bell mimicked vocal cords. After the telephone had made him rich, he moved into new fields where he broke the rules again. He constructed massive kites that could carry a man aloft, built hydrofoil boats, and improved the phonograph. He never let expertise or age stop him from innovating.

Lack of maturity, education, or experience isn't a problem either. Those with less experience repeatedly succeed where their more enlightened contemporaries fail. They should, because they have a big advantage—their mental ruts are not as deep.

Einstein Thinking is not a complex process. But it isn't easy. It is like writing with the wrong hand. It feels strange to write your name using your left hand if you are right-handed and vice versa. You want to switch back to the usual way—the comfortable way—as soon as possible. Einstein Thinking feels the same way. You must consider ideas that common sense will scream are absurd. You will break cherished rules, violate sacred precedents, think heretical thoughts. Fortunately, if you are in the right mood, it can be lots of fun. Einstein's "ambidextrous" thinking changed the world. Thinking more like Einstein can change your life.

Einstein Thinking is a collection of techniques that mimic Einstein's approach to problem solving. It supports targeting real problems, breaking patterns, breaking rules, growing infant ideas, and other habits that were natural to Einstein.

EINSTEIN THINKING

"Sometimes one pays the most for the things one gets for nothing."

—ALBERT EINSTEIN

From Einstein's comments, we know what he felt was important when solving problems. The rule-breaking techniques that Einstein used instinctively are techniques that anyone can mimic. By doing what he did, even those of us with more modest intelligence can think like Einstein. The process consists of four basic steps.

Finding the Right Problem

Even Einstein couldn't find a solution if he had the wrong problem. You must have an enabling problem, a problem that allows imaginative solutions different from your original expectations. Disabling problems have so many restrictions they only can be solved by impossible tasks. A disabling problem would be: "I want to fly by flapping my arms like wings." An enabling problem would allow any solution that got your feet off the ground. A good problem expands options. Finding the right problem requires much thought, especially when the solution seems obvious.

Breaking the Pattern

Einstein was most successful when he was willing to consider anything, particularly ridiculous ideas. Breaking patterns tears you out of your rut by generating the novel ideas that you are usually too practical to consider.

Breaking Rules

Rule breaking is a focused, deliberate way of finding solutions. If you have been unable to find a solution among all the acceptable alternatives, then you must examine the impossible alternatives—you must break some rules.

Grow the Solution

It took Einstein years before he could develop relativity into a useful theory. Great solutions seldom seem great when conceived. Compared with existing ideas, even the best breakthroughs seem inferior. You must suspend judgment, get help, and make mistakes to grow an idea into a great solution.

Einstein naturally used these techniques to change our world. He used a more enabling problem. He played with wild notions. He broke a specific rule. And then he developed the idea that came from breaking rules until it was a superior solution. You can tackle your problems the same way.

EINSTEIN'S THINKING FORMULAS

"The hardest thing in the world to understand is the income tax."

—ALBERT EINSTEIN

Einstein didn't need help to think like Einstein. It was natural. But thinking like Einstein isn't natural to us. We need help. We will use formulas and forms to mimic Einstein's thinking. This seems counterintuitive. Formulas are rules. Why constrict your thinking with a formula when you are trying to break rules?

Einstein Thinking uses the structure of formulas to redirect the flow of your thoughts. If you wanted to redirect the course of a river, you would not let nature take its course. Something must channel it. Redirecting your thinking requires structure too. You must use the formulas until you have escaped your rule rut. Even Einstein could have used a formula to force him out of the "uncertainty" rut that shut down his creativity.

These formulas for creative thinking are modeled in a series of forms. Completing them will force you through exercises that will liberate your thinking from your rule ruts. Blank copies of the forms are in Appendix A, or you can easily draw them in a notebook.

Use the forms to create solutions that you would normally not even consider. In the example in Figure 2.1, forms could lead you to posting an official-looking sign prohibiting food in the area, promising to pay a colleague twenty dollars for every doughnut you eat, or anonymously announcing that there are doughnuts in your area and that everyone in the building should come and have two.

If you are stuck in a rule rut, use the forms to drag yourself out. As you rewire your brain to regularly break your rules, you can rely less on the forms. Apply them as needed to keep track of ideas or break through

Problem Definition		
Avoid eating doughnuts at work.		
Idea	**Reasons idea will work**	**Reasons idea won't work**
Blow up the doughnut shop around the corner.	I can resist the doughnuts if they aren't in the building.	Someone will bring them from somewhere else.
Put land mines around the doughnuts.	I won't eat doughnuts if I am afraid to.	Doughnuts are not frightening.
Threaten to maim my colleagues who bring doughnuts unless they stop.	If no one brings doughnuts, I can't eat them.	I can't stop people from bringing doughnuts.

Rules	**Violate the Rule**	**Circumvent the Rule**	**Opposite Rule**	**Special Case**
I can't keep doughnuts out of the building.				X
I'm not afraid of doughnuts.			X	
I can't stop people from bringing doughnuts.		X		

Figure 2.1: The Doughnut Problem

obstacles. But if you are having fun and the ideas are flowing, a blank sheet of paper or tape recorder are perfect for capturing your insights.

We will show you the steps of Einstein Thinking sequentially. However, you don't have to solve your problems this way. Defining a problem may lead you directly to an idea you can grow to a solution, or discovering a rule that must be broken could lead to more creative pattern breaking. Think like Einstein as a way to break your current rules, not to create new ones.

THE BEST PROBLEMS FOR EINSTEIN THINKING

"When the solution is simple, God is answering."

—ALBERT EINSTEIN

In the next chapters, we will start thinking like Einstein to solve tough problems. Rule breaking can be a one-shot idea generation technique, but we will examine creating significant solutions first. Select a tough problem to solve. Einstein Thinking is most useful when the current solutions aren't working. You must break the rules because there is no other solution. Such problems have the greatest motivation too—the rewards are greater and the consequences more dire. Einstein solved the two toughest problems in physics in one year by breaking the rules. See what rule breaking can do for your toughest problem.

Great solutions require a more in-depth application of Einstein Thinking. You may need to repeat the process several times. There will be dead ends and new problem definitions. Mistakes are vital; you are not covering new ground unless you make mistakes.

After you have a better understanding of rule breaking in problem solving, we will use this process for smaller problems. Thinking like Einstein is not needed to solve all problems, but any problem can benefit from it. It doesn't hurt to break the rules for mundane needs. There is always a better way, but improvements are seldom sought when the existing solution works. And breaking rules keeps your mind in shape, a great reason to use this new way of thinking on ordinary problems.

There can be numerous variations on these techniques. Even Einstein can be improved upon. Create some for yourself. Get into the habit of looking for a better idea because the world needs more good solutions.

CHAPTER THREE

The Right Problem

"The significant problems
we face cannot be solved
at the same level of
thinking we were at when
we created them."

—ALBERT EINSTEIN

When Einstein began working on relativity and the solution that ultimately became $E = mc^2$, he had a big advantage—he had a good problem.
Many of Einstein's contemporaries had been working on the same phenomena, but they were trying to solve a very different problem. Their
problem went something like this:

"How can nature appear to act that way when we know that it can't?"

They did not succeed. More experiments, more money, or more effort
would not have helped. They failed because they were looking for an
answer that did not exist. Einstein succeeded because he was working on
a problem that enabled a solution. He asked himself:

"What would nature be like if it did act the way we observe it to act?"

This problem has a solution. Einstein found it, and it changed our
world. But even the great Einstein would have failed if he had pursued the
wrong problem. The first step in thinking like Einstein is to form a problem that enables you to seek and recognize a solution.

ANSWERS NEED QUESTIONS

"In the fields of observation, chance favors only the prepared mind."

—PASTEUR

Answers are not answers without questions. We find answers, and solutions, because we have good questions. Consider Figure 3.1.

There doesn't seem to be much in common between items on the first list. But they are all related answers—you just don't know the questions.

All of the answers dealt with political aspects of mining. But that is hard to discern without knowing the questions. You cannot identify answers without the right questions. And without a good problem, it is hard to spot even an obvious solution.

Solving a problem is like looking for valuable antiques. You will find only junk unless you know what you are looking for. Great new ideas are too different from our current thinking, and too similar to nonsolutions to be casually recognized. But when we know what to look for, the probability of finding a great solution soars.

The ancient genius Archimedes took baths all of his life, and each time he entered the bath, the water rose. But only when he was looking for a way to measure the volume of the king's crown did he recognize the rising water as a brilliant volume-measuring solution. He was so excited that he ran naked from the bath. To find a breakthrough that exciting, you must have a clear vision of the solution that you are seeking. Then you too can recognize your answer when you step into it.

WRITE IT DOWN

"The illiterate of the twenty-first century will not be those who cannot read and write, but those who cannot learn, unlearn, and relearn."

—ALVIN TOFFLER, AUTHOR OF *FUTURE SHOCK*

Great problems have many distinguishing characteristics, but they start with a permanent record. You must write a problem down. There is

A List
Herbert Hoover
Permanent South Pole Station
Belgium Congo

Mining and Politics in the Twentieth Century	
Herbert Hoover	What renowned mining engineer became president of the United States?
Permanent South Pole Station	What scientific project has been key to limiting mineral claims in Antarctica?
Belgium Congo	Concerns over Nazi control of uranium supplies in which country led to Albert Einstein's sending Franklin Roosevelt a letter advising an atomic weapons program?

Figure 3.1: Answers Need Questions

something about recording thoughts that gives them life. Unless you are faced with immediate death, write out a problem statement to solve a tough problem.

A problem statement focuses your mind. Just as the focused beam of a laser can slice through metal, your mind can slice through the toughest problems if it is focused. Your problem statement is that focus.

You will be tempted not to do this exercise. You may be thinking, "I know this problem, I don't need to write it down." You would rather just read on. Don't even think about it. It won't work. You must write out problems in order to work out brilliant solutions.

Begin with a brief problem statement. Condense it to those few nouns and verbs that are essential to the problem. Use twenty-five words or less. Even the most difficult problems can be expressed in twenty-five words. Any description beyond a few essential points is more likely to drag some of the very rules that are preventing a solution into the problem. After describing the problem, briefly record why it must be solved. Problems with compelling needs get solved. If you don't need to solve it, it isn't really a problem.

Problem	Why It MUST Be Solved	Next Step
Reduce product returns	Wiping out product margins	Identify top three reasons for returns
Make more money	Pay for the kids' college	Ask for raise
Increase European sales 3X	Economies of scale too low to be profitable	Increase Munich sales force
Eliminate hunger	Because there is enough food, hunger is repugnant	Einstein Thinking analysis
Roof leaks	Ruining ceiling, carpet	Replace shingles

Figure 3.2: Write It Down

Finally, record a next step for each problem. Some problems suffer more from a lack of effort than from a lack of solutions. We solve the problems that we work to solve. Even misdirected efforts are not wasted. Mistakes, errors, and wrong turns are crucial to finding solutions. If you are not following through with the next step on a problem, you need motivation more than a creative solution.

If you have multiple problems you want solved, record them even if you can't consciously work on all of them. Just reviewing a problem list regularly will inspire interesting ideas. Most problems suffer from a lack of attention. We don't give difficult problems enough attention to spark a solution. But our brains can work on problems around the clock, regardless of whatever else we might be doing. The mind just needs to know that you want a solution. When you think about a problem regularly, even if it is only a brief review, your brain is reminded that the solution is needed. Your neurons will fire away until eventually you find some answers. The brilliant mathematical genius Maria Agnesi would frequently awake with the answer to a problem. After detailing the solution, she went back to sleep. She was often surprised to find a solution by her bed in the morning. Madame C.J. Walker became America's first self-made woman millionaire in the same way. She dreamed the hair-growth formula that she needed to create her fortune.

If you haven't already done so, go to Appendix A, "Einstein Thinking Forms." Describe a few of the problems you would like to solve, along with the reason you want a solution and a next step. After you have completed your list, select one problem to solve thinking like Einstein. Hard problems are best. Their solutions are most likely obscured by a stupid rule. Select one problem to actively focus your attention on. We will develop this problem step-by-step into an enabling problem statement. I will use eliminating hunger as an example.

Step 1: Initial Problem Definition (Twenty-five words or less)	Eliminate hunger

CREATING AN ENABLING PROBLEM

"Perfection of means and confusion of ends seem to characterize our age."
—ALBERT EINSTEIN

No problem is impossible to solve, although some tasks may be impossible to do. You may think you need to do the impossible, like create a new product line overnight or build a factory in a week. If so, you have the wrong problem. Bad problems seem unattainable. Good problems enable great solutions. Your next step in creating a great solution is to craft an enabling problem.

Structure your problem so that you can find answers, as many and varied answers as possible. Good problems seek to satisfy real needs. Bad problems specify explicit solutions. If an explicit solution is impractical, you are stuck. Good problems allow for trade-offs. Bad problems are inflexible.

You can never tell where your solution will be found, or how you will ultimately stumble across it. An enabling problem allows you to pursue solutions in many directions, particularly those you don't think will work.

Suppose you had been given a problem like the following to solve:

Bob needs more boxes to ship his apples to market. He has rectangular pieces of cardboard, one-by-two meters in size. What is the biggest box Bob can form from the cardboard to ship his apples to market?

This is not a good problem. The only way to solve this problem is to calculate how to make the biggest cardboard boxes. The answer seems almost built in. This is fine when the built-in answer works. But pat answers usually don't work for tough problems like the one you are trying to solve.

Einstein had the peculiar habit of attacking a problem by going back to the basics. He dispensed with most of the known facts, deriving the key concepts himself from scratch. By doing so, he avoided many of the bad assumptions that confused his colleagues. You can use this same technique to make your problem an enabling problem.

Identify the Real Issues

"A man always has two reasons for what he does—a good one, and the real one."

—J. P. MORGAN

All problems exist in a hierarchy of needs. Every problem is driven by higher-level needs—the reasons for seeking a solution. People solve problems to get rich, continue eating, or show a great aunt that they could amount to something. But these higher-level needs are often ignored in problem solving.

You selected your target problem because you believe it is the way to meet some higher-level needs. Your target problem may be the answer. But there may also be other, better ways to meet your higher-level needs. Perhaps the higher-level need is your real issue. Your problem statement may be driven by an outdated rule that this is the only way to satisfy your higher-level need. Making the higher-level need the target problem can open up many new possible solutions.

Our apple farm question presupposes that Bob should turn the rectangles of cardboard into boxes of maximum volume for shipping apples. Shipping more apples to market may be only a small part of Bob's problem hierarchy.

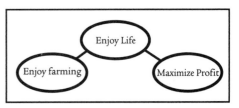

Figure 3.3: Bob's Basic Needs

To find a real solution, we need to begin at the basics, with Bob.

If we interviewed Bob, we may find that he really wants to enjoy life. This shouldn't be a surprise. As we delve deeper, we find that Bob believes he can enjoy life more if he enjoys farming more, or if he made more money.

If Bob was really interested in maximizing his profit, his problem statement should read something like this: *Bob has grown more apples than he has boxes for shipping them to market. He also has five hundred one-by-two meter cardboard pieces. Maximize Bob's profit.*

This statement of the same problem leaves open new possibilities. Bob could form the cardboard into fancy cones or pyramids. Though less voluminous, the new packages may greatly enhance the appearance and value of the apples. There are other solutions that have nothing to do with packages. Perhaps instead of a shipping box problem, Bob has valuable information about an oversupply of apples. Instead of wasting his time packaging apples that will command a poor price because of the glut, Bob should be shorting apple futures, something that may earn him far more.

But another core problem was how to enjoy farming more. Bob may want to establish his apples as the world's finest. Or he may have more fun making apple cider. Bob's seemingly

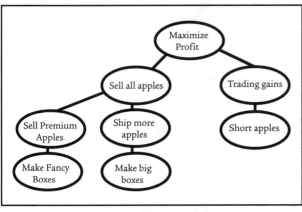

Figure 3.4: Bob's New Solutions

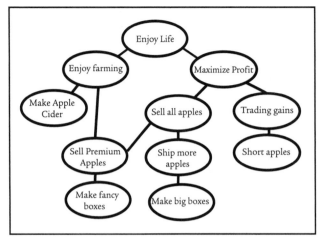

Figure 3.5: Bob's New Big Picture

simple apple-boxing problem can expand to allow for multitudes of new solutions. By returning to the basics of the problem, we greatly expanded the possible solutions and made finding a solution much more interesting.

Problem statements should list the desired ends, not the means. Problem statements that dictate the solution make it hard to break the rules. And to think like Einstein, you've got to break the rules.

Step 2: Problem Hierarchy	
Higher-level need	Eliminate poverty
Is this the real problem?	Eliminate hunger
Self-problems	Eliminate barriers to initiative

Before you attempt to solve any target problem, explore the needs that mandate a solution. Start by identifying those needs. Record them. I like to draw a chart showing how a need spawns other needs to help me understand my problem hierarchy. I draw my target problem in the center of the page. The needs that drive it go above it. I record alternate problems/solutions as appropriate on the chart. Lines connect problems to their solutions, which are also problems.

You may also want to write down what you believe the sub-problems to be, but don't focus on them except to determine if there is a single, intractable, lower-level problem at the root of your bigger problem. It is easier to create innovative solutions as you focus on higher levels of the problem hierarchy.

Describe your own hierarchy in any way you want, as long as there is a physical record. Identify the needs and problems that are creating your target problem. Then consider if the higher-level need is the real problem you must address.

Ignore Limitations

"Do not quench your inspiration and your imagination;
do not become the slave of your model."

—VINCENT VAN GOGH

Einstein rarely let established ideas limit his freedom to consider new solutions. He even ignored his own theories. If you are to solve your impossible problem, you must ignore your limitations too. Forget that there isn't enough time or money. There never is. Forget about egos, attitudes, or tradition. You can't solve the problem if you let these obstacles get in the way.

The next step in creating an enabling problem statement is to identify the limitations and ignore them. If your definition of the problem assumes that money or time is a limitation, remove them. Don't consider them as you look for a solution. It is not easy to do, but it is key to solving problems.

Step 3: Ignore Limitations	
Is money limiting?	Money limits
Is someone's ego limiting?	
Is fear limiting?	
Is knowledge limiting?	
Is red tape limiting?	Red tape limits
Is skill limiting?	
Is schedule limiting?	
Is education or credentials limiting?	
Is commitment limiting?	
Is attitude limiting?	People are selfish. "Haves" are cynical.

Write down everything you believe will limit you in creating a great solution to your target problem. Then forget them. We will address these limitations later in a chapter on rule breaking. But for now, they don't exist.

Eliminate Old Answers

"Mere precedent is a dangerous source of authority."

—ANDREW JACKSON

Tolerable solutions and an "if it isn't broken, don't fix it" attitude will often prevent you from considering better solutions. If you start thinking this way, give yourself a mental shake and remember that good ideas are the greatest obstacles great ideas have to overcome. Newtonian physics effectively blocked many refinements to our knowledge of the universe— i.e., Einstein's theory of relativity—because it worked so well. There was no reason to question it because it almost always worked.

Solutions that have been kicked around for years should be temporarily off-limits in defining your problem. This may seem to contradict the notion of broadening your solution options. But these solutions are not new, and you are only excluding them until you can examine a new set of answers without prejudice. You must ignore old answers for now so they don't mislead you. If they were a real solution to the problem, then your problem would already be solved.

Step 4: Ignore Old Answers	
List, then ignore your current top three solutions	1. Food Aid
	2. Developement programs
	3. Immigration

To free yourself to think about better alternatives, identify your current top three solutions. They are now off-limits. You can't break rules and cling to your rule rut at the same time.

Simplify

"Things should be made as simple as possible, but not any simpler."

—ALBERT EINSTEIN

Simple, spare problems should be easiest to solve. Einstein simplified his problems. He developed his Special Theory of Relativity first. It was special in the sense that it applied to a simple set of cases. A more accurate name would have been the Simple Theory of Relativity. Working on a simpler problem helped Einstein develop the ideas and tools that made a more general theory possible.

Many people are reluctant to simplify a problem because it seems like cheating. It is. You are trying to break the rules that are making your problem impossible, and simplifying the problem is an important step.

Step 5: Simplify	
Define a simpler version of a problem	Eliminate barriers to prosperity

Eliminate everything you can from your problem statement. Remove preconditions, half-solutions, and excess words. Free it from the baggage that makes a solution so difficult. Einstein once declared in a lecture that the laws of physics should be simple. When asked what he would do if they weren't, he replied, "Then I would not be interested in them." Focus your interest on a simple problem.

MOTIVATION

"Nothing truly valuable arises from ambition or from a mere sense of duty."

—ALBERT EINSTEIN

Great ideas are great because they are needed. We need compelling reasons to consider uncomfortable, fresh ideas. Finding a solution must be important enough to overcome our mental and physical inertia. That is why they say that necessity is the mother of invention. If there is a need, a solution can be found.

The Christmas hymn "Silent Night" was written because a church organ was broken. Only a guitar would be available for Christmas services. Consequently, a beautiful hymn was composed that could be sung with a guitar for accompaniment.

Another genius, Stephen Hawking, claimed he embarked on his physics career because he met a nice girl and wanted to get married. He needed a good job to do so. Hawking unraveled the secrets of the universe to support a family.

James Spangler invented what became Hoover vacuum cleaners because he wanted to keep his janitorial job. He was too old to lift the heavy carpet-cleaning machine, which also kicked up dust that made him violently sick. Spangler would have to quit his job, something that he could not afford to do, unless he could find another way to clean carpets. He did.

J.C. Hallmark helped reinvent the American greeting card business because he had to. Like other card distributors, he was in the business of importing elegantly engraved cards from Europe for Valentine's Day and Christmas. But Hallmark's entire inventory of cards was destroyed in a fire weeks before Valentine's Day. It was too late to get more cards from Europe. Facing financial ruin, Hallmark bought a small engraving firm and began producing simple designs. And since he now owned his own press, he started producing more casual cards for other occasions to keep his press running. Because he had no choice, Hallmark changed his industry.

You will be much more inventive if your need is great. Imagine a simple problem like cleaning out a closet. It has been impossible to clean. But if you were to be executed in two weeks unless you cleaned the closet, you would do it. Or if you were to be rewarded with $100,000 dollars for cleaning the closet, you would do the job. And you can solve vastly more difficult problems with the right incentives.

Hernan Cortez was a master of motivation. He used the trick of cutting off retreat, destroying his own fleet, and stranding his army in hostile territory. But he was equally skillful at creating carrots to entice his small army. Cortez promised fortunes in treasure to lure an army to Mexico. The men who followed him wanted to become fabulously rich, so rich that it was worth years of toil, deprivation, and risk of death in a strange land. He was so convincing that the island of Cuba was deserted by most of its Spanish settlers, who left to join Cortez's expedition.

Cortez provided motivations that were not abstract. Those that followed him had a clear picture in their minds of what success would bring. They saw themselves as lords of vast estates, receiving obsequious guests beneath regal coats of arms. They anticipated wenching and gluttony. The masses they would buy to assure the salvation of their souls gave them great comfort. They saw their portraits hung in great halls, honored and respected for generations by noble descendants. It was gloriously compelling enough to brave real torture, pain, and death.

Motivated by Cortez's carrot-on-a-stick, his army found a way to conquer. They didn't do it solely by strength of arms, nor did they do it alone. Cortez picked his way through complex linguistic and diplomatic problems to win many battles without any physical fighting. He convinced many powerful vassal states that they could throw off Aztec oppression by following him. It was never easy and never pretty, but Cortez and his men found the solutions. They had everything to gain, and everything to lose. It is too bad that Cortez was not looking for a cure for cancer.

You must create rewards and consequences that will motivate you to find solutions. After defining the problem you want solved, specify what you will gain if you succeed. It must excite you, thrill you. You should want to continue work on a solution whenever you can. Problems with compelling carrots get solved.

Your motivation cannot just be abstract words on a page. Picture yourself running your division, receiving that prestigious award, enjoying the fruits of your success. Your vision must be tangible enough to inspire you when your problem seems impossible. It must capture all that finding the solution will mean to you. Words will not motivate you to do the impossible. An emotion-charged vision will. Describe that vision.

Step 6: Carrots	
What good will come of a solution?	Peace
	Guilt-free prosperity

The consequences of failure should be equally compelling. How will you feel if you are beaten? How will you suffer? Think of the regrets, the disappointment, perhaps even the real physical pain. Make the image real and frightening. And, of course, record your images so they can be quickly recalled.

Step 7: Sticks	
What will happen if there is no solution?	War
	Epidemics
	Environmental disaster
	Guilt

Until your carrots and sticks are compelling enough, you will not solve your problem. Motivation precedes resolution.

Re-size the Problem

"When a man knows he is to be hanged in a fortnight, it concentrates his mind wonderfully."

—SAMUEL JOHNSON

If you have not created sufficient motivation to solve your problem, it may be too big or too small. Small problems often fester for years because the short-term cost of fixing them is more than the short-term pain of leaving them unsolved. We give up on big problems because they are too hard. You may need to re-size your problem in order to solve it.

Make a small problem bigger so that it gets the attention it needs now. You will be more creative and persistent in finding solutions to many of the nuisances in your life if you can artificially increase your need. Make your little problem a bigger problem. Invent the worst possible consequences for failure. Revel in the pain you will feel if it is not solved. Then solve it.

Big problems are also difficult. We give up before we start. The dire consequence seems inevitable. Even enormous rewards seem unreachable. You are as likely to attempt to leap across the Grand Canyon as really try to solve an impossible problem.

Reduce your big problem to something you can solve. Other people use this strategy on us all the time. They say, "It won't be hard," or, "Just a few hours." Right! They are trying to scale the problem to something manageable. They have the right idea. You must believe whatever they want you to do is attainable, or you won't try.

To reduce a tough problem to a practical first step, you must resolve that first intermediate issue. And when that is done, tackle the next intermediate solution. Develop motivations for these intermediate solutions. Make a 20 percent solution interesting.

Ancient Chinese generals had a wonderful motivational tactic. They would put soldiers in a position where retreat was absolutely impossible. They had only two options—fight and prevail, or die. The men fought like dragons. Increase your motivation by putting yourself in a more desperate situation. Make a large wager that you will take an intermediate action. Arrange for the moral equivalent of hanging if you fail. You will find your ability to focus on the interim solution immeasurably enhanced.

Step 8: Size	
Shrink or expand the problem to encourage action	Foster universal prosperity. Eliminate hunger in a neighborhood.

Evaluate Your Motivation

"Where the willingness is great, the difficulties cannot be."

— NICCOLO MACHIAVELLI

The final check for your problem statement and motivation is asking yourself:

▶ Do I believe this problem can be solved?
▶ Can I solve it?
▶ Will I enjoy solving it?

If the answer to any of these questions is no, then something must change. Otherwise, your lack of conviction or distaste for the problem will sabotage your efforts.

Step 9: Is the problem compelling and fun?	**Yes!!!**

We humans have a poor record of succeeding at anything we believe to be impossible. But there is also a remarkable record of people doing the impossible when they didn't know it was impossible. It is much the same with problems we think we will enjoy—they get solved. You will stack the deck in your favor if you believe that the problem can be solved and that you will enjoy it.

Continue working on your motivations until you feel committed to spending the time and energy needed to find a solution. If you can't create sufficient motivation, start over on your problem statement. Don't even try to solve your problem if it is not compelling. My rule of thumb is that a problem is compelling if you think about it before breakfast. And, if you remember it when the alarm clock goes off, you are truly motivated.

If you can't create sufficient motivation, you have two choices: abandon the problem, or create a new attitude.

New Attitude

"Be careful what you pretend to be because you are what you pretend to be."

—KURT VONNEGUT

If you are still certain that you have the right problem, and that it can't be solved, there is only one other thing to change—your attitude.

You may need to find the right mask to hide behind, the right alter ego. Alter egos are often more successful because they lack the limitations that were getting in our way. Since it is not us, it need not have our weaknesses. Fictional characters like Don Quixote or Dr. Jekyl used masquerades and alter egos to do things that they otherwise could not or would not do. For extraordinary results and temporary fun, construct your own alter ego.

Take out a clean sheet of paper. On the top, create a name for your alter ego. It can be forceful, mysterious, or whimsical, depending on your alter ego's mission. You may wish to append one or more appropriate titles of accomplishment or nobility.

Next, describe this person. Is she authoritative, strong, intelligent? Describe why she wants to solve your problem. Feel free to borrow characteristics liberally from people that you admire. Details are important if your alter ego and her passions and strengths are going to be real to you. The car she drives, books she reads, or weekend plans are all relevant. Create a complete picture.

Try imagining that this person you have created suddenly became conscious in your body. What would she do right now? How will she solve the problem? Write all of these things down. Since your alter ego is using your circumstances to do all of this, you could do it too. So why not you?

This exercise removes yourself from your self-imposed limitations by removing you from yourself. Don't develop a psychiatric disorder, but convince yourself that your problem can be solved.

Focus: The Ubiquitous Problem

"I've given up trying to be rigorous. All I'm concerned about is being right."
—Stephen Hawking

After you have defined a motivating, enabling problem, you may still need to go through the steps of defining your problem several times before you are satisfied. Doing so is important and invaluable. You will find there are many more sides to the problem than you first supposed. Each new point of view broadens your accessible solutions.

Step 10: Problem Definition	Eliminate barriers to properity.

Difficult problems require long, focused effort. A problem statement provides a consistent focal point for directing efforts toward finding a solution. Problems that are written down and reviewed are ten times more likely to be solved. Those that consume one's thoughts throughout the day are a hundred times more likely to be solved.

Charles Goodyear is a classic example of what happens when you are focused. Goodyear played a key role in making rubber commercially viable. But he is the last person that one would expect to have done it. When he started his crusade to make rubber a viable product, Goodyear knew nothing about chemistry or chemical manufacturing. He had no money or business experience. But Goodyear had one unbeatable advantage—he was obsessed. He was determined to commercialize rubber. Even when he and his family were living in a derelict rubber factory, eating off rubber plates, and probably wishing that rubber was edible, Goodyear remained committed. He never let up. He had numerous failures, but Goodyear stayed focused on finding a way to make viable rubber. He ultimately succeeded, stumbling across the vulcanizing process that solved his problem, and made himself and his long-suffering family wealthy.

After you have defined a firm idea of the solution you want, your mind will be able to focus its incredible problem-solving power on that solution. It is important that you see your problem definition often. Make it ubiquitous. Put a copy in your notebook or planner. Post a short summary of the problem or a code word representing it in a conspicuous place, like the dashboard of your car. Whenever you are reminded of the problem, think of the carrots and sticks. Motivation will lead to better thinking. Defining a problem clearly and thinking of it often is enough to stimulate good ideas from within your current patterns of thinking.

As you generate new ideas, you may want to change the definition of the problem. Climbing out of your mental rut will give you a new perspective on your problem. Changing the problem is good as long as you have one problem statement to keep your mind focused. An enabling problem statement is key to finding your solution.

CHAPTER FOUR

No Bad
Ideas

> "If we knew what we were doing, it would not be called research, would it?"
>
> —ALBERT EINSTEIN

People worry about creating stupid ideas, so they develop concepts using old thinking that hasn't worked, but sounds sensible. This is a good way to avoid ridicule, but a bad way to solve problems. To create a brilliant solution, you need new ideas. And most will sound absolutely stupid.

Thinking like Einstein generates lots of mistakes, weird notions, and dead ends along with good ideas. The bad ideas are almost as useful as the good ones. I like to call bad ideas "Chris Concepts" in honor of one of history's craziest ideas—which turned out to be enormously important.

CHRIS CONCEPTS

> *"History is a lie agreed upon."*
>
> —NAPOLEON BONAPARTE

The story you learned about Christopher Columbus was backwards. Columbus was the guy that had it wrong. There was a good reason that everyone laughed at him. Christopher Columbus wanted to sail west to Asia. It was an incredibly stupid idea. The leading navigators and scientists knew that the earth was round. But they also knew that Asia was much too far away to be reached by sailing west. Fifteenth century boats were incapable of making the journey. If it hadn't been for the totally unexpected intervention of the Americas, Columbus and his crews would have died at sea somewhere southeast of Hawaii.

Columbus had the facts all wrong. But Columbus's idea, wrong as it was, did get him out of a centuries-old rut. When he was finally given the resources to test his idea, he made a brilliant discovery. It was not the discovery he wanted to make, or thought he had made, but it was still important.

In later years, people sanitized the Columbus story so that it was Christopher the man with the facts and the clear vision that made the important discovery. But actually it was Columbus the man with more courage than good data that changed the world.

All bad ideas are potential Chris Concepts. They may not be the solution that you are looking for, but they could still carry you forward to a solution that no one has even imagined. Chris Concepts are valuable. Create as many of them as you can. Don't hold back because your ideas seem dumb.

THE MORLEY-MICHELSON FAILURE

"Logic: The art of thinking and reasoning in strict accordance with the limitations of human misunderstanding."

—AMBROSE BIERCE

Some ideas seem to be failures when they are really huge signposts pointing at a breakthrough. A "failed" idea played a key role in Einstein's discovery of relativity. When Einstein made his breakthrough discovery of relativity, he relied heavily on a "failed" experiment. In 1887, A.A. Michelson and E.W. Morley set out to measure the change in the speed of light. This change was an important prediction of the current physics theories. They devised a brilliant experiment to show that light moving counter to the earth's motion traveled more slowly than light moving across the earth's path. It required a very large and ingenious device. Finally, after months of careful preparation, they were ready. They expected to become famous, be invited to all the right parties, and die content that physics students forever after would be forced to learn about their brilliance.

But something went very wrong. Their clever experiment could detect no change in the speed of light. It was viewed as a failure. Michelson and Morley didn't pursue it any further. Of course, they had uncovered the big clue—light always goes the same speed. It allowed Einstein to discover the principles of relativity years later. Michelson and Morley might have been as famous as Einstein, if they had recognized their mistake as the breakthrough it really was.

WILDLY SUCCESSFUL BAD IDEAS

"The only man who never makes a mistake is the man who never does anything."
—THEODORE ROOSEVELT

Bad ideas, or Chris Concepts, are essential to developing good solutions. Innovation is rarely a direct line from problem to solution. The path to a great solution twists, turns, and doubles back. Along the way there are many failures that are essential to developing the final solution. It would be nice to avoid all the Chris Concepts between the problem and solution, but one is rarely so lucky.

Chris Concepts were key to most of history's greatest discoveries. Alexander Fleming got excited when he noticed that tears inhibited the growth of bacteria. He tried and failed to develop a medicinal use for tears. But the idea sensitized him to an important idea—that certain substances could kill harmful bacteria without injuring the patient.

When Fleming found certain molds that inhibited bacterial growth, he recognized the importance immediately. This discovery led to penicillin, which has saved millions. It has been the single most important medical advance in history—and it started with a bad idea.

Put the Statue of Liberty in Egypt? That was original plan. It was supposed to be a lighthouse for the Suez Canal. Auguste Bartholdi worked on the project for years. The design was completed, but it was never built because of a shortage of funds. The monumental artistic and design work that went into it seemed like a terrible waste, until the right opportunity came along. And suddenly the idea became wildly successful and famous.

Neighbors ridiculed Gail Borden for his idea of moving the entire population of Galveston, Texas, into a cooled building to "freeze out disease." Anyone who has lived near Galveston knows that this was not a stupid idea, but it was years before it was practical. However, Borden's idea sensitized him to preventing disease by preventing spoilage. Years later, he was crossing the Atlantic when several children on the ship died from spoiled milk. Borden became determined to prevent illness caused by spoiled dairy products and revolutionized the dairy industry by condensing and canning milk.

Bad ideas are still blossoming. Not too many years ago, videotext was dying before most people knew it had been around. If you don't remember videotext, it was news, shopping, weather, etc., available via your television. Another Chris Concept? Just ask some of the early videotext pioneers who became billionaires by rolling videotext business savvy onto the Internet.

Don't Abandon New Thinking

"The most incomprehensible thing about the world is that it is comprehensible."

—ALBERT EINSTEIN

Even new thinking that is demonstrably inferior to your current solutions shouldn't be abandoned. Current solutions can hit a dead end. Progress may someday be in the direction of these formerly inferior solutions.

At the beginning of the age of exploration, the greatest seafaring nation in the world was China. China had a huge navy. Their massive ships were centuries ahead of European technology. Chinese merchants plied trade routes all over the South Pacific and Indian Oceans. The Chinese Admiral Cheng Ho led many expeditions that visited and charted ports as far as the East Coast of Africa. China was well on its way to becoming the preeminent nation in the world.

Unfortunately, Chinese leaders learned the wrong things from Cheng Ho's expeditions. They concluded that they had nothing to learn from the outside world because outside technology, products, and societies were so obviously inferior to their own. China banned foreign travel and let its navy and merchant marine rot in port. Much smaller and less advanced nations like Portugal, Spain, England, and even the tiny Netherlands vigorously pursued seaborne trade and exploration. It took centuries for them to catch up to where China had been, but they did. And they came to dominate the world, including controlling much of China.

A bad idea can be like collodion. Collodion was a first aid product commonly used in the nineteenth century. It didn't do any medical good. It was poisonous. But everyone thought it was a good thing to put on cuts. It was often handy in the workshop, where it might be applied to a cut on the hand of a would-be inventor. Purely by chance, collodion was instrumental in the invention of safety glass, celluloid, rayon, and blasting caps. It was just there, got mixed up in things, and proved to be a solution. Chris Concepts can be just like collodion. They may not be useful for any intended solution. But, if they hang around long enough, they may be the catalyst for a real breakthrough.

Brains don't have capacity limits. Nor do brains seem to have any difficulty considering numerous options in parallel. One can't have too many ideas to draw from. Today's Chris Concept can easily be tomorrow's mother lode.

Bauxite is a classic example of a bad idea whose time finally came. Aluminum is refined from bauxite ore. It is extremely plentiful. For years, miners found numerous deposits of the stuff. They ignored it. Only a fool would stake a bauxite claim. Unrefined bauxite is worthless, and extracting even minute quantities of aluminum was staggeringly expensive. Aluminum was the most precious of precious metals, trimming the crowns of emperors and capping the Washington monument, and bauxite was the most worthless of ores. Then, it was discovered how to refine aluminum from bauxite using an electric current. The process was cheap, and became even cheaper. Suddenly, bauxite was a very good idea and aluminum became so common that we now throw it away. Rich bauxite deposits are eagerly sought and developed. Bauxite is now a great solution.

RECORDING YOUR IDEAS

"Life is too important to be taken seriously."

—OSCAR WILDE

Recording all your ideas is vitally important. Otherwise, the many Chris Concepts you create will wither away. Recording bad ideas keeps them around so you can use them in the future. And recording your ideas is essential for your brilliant thinking as well. The way that history repeats itself demonstrates that the same good ideas will pop up independently in many places. The creator most likely to develop the idea into a solution—and to get the credit—is the person who records his idea.

Record each idea on the Ideas Synthesis Form in the back of this book, or something similar to it. Over time you will need to move to a notebook to keep up with your creations.

Don't evaluate your ideas as you create them, just list them. Fill in the "Reasons Idea Will Work" and "Reasons Idea Won't Work" columns later. Writing your ideas and reviewing them later will help stimulate more thinking. Record all linkages to other ideas and thoughts too. Einstein Thinking builds your personal reservoir of ideas, relations, and analogies, the raw material of more ideas.

Idea	Reasons Idea Will Work	Reasons Idea Won't Work
Turn the world vegetarian	Will increase available foodstuffs	Difficult to change behavior
Impose a hunger tax on luxuries	Puts burden on those most able to bear it	Rich nations won't support
Breed aggressive urban crops	Food is needed in poor cities	Urban environment too harsh
Eliminate taxes on food production	Encourage more food production	Poor nations tax all economic activity

Figure 4.1: Sample Idea Synthesis Form

New thinking doesn't spring from nothing. Considering a new concept, even if it isn't a solution, creates ideas that can be used in the future. Use your list of ideas as a problem solving tool kit. Use this collection of Chris Concepts to inspire other ideas and solutions.

MORE IS BETTER

"I haven't failed. I've found ten thousand ways that don't work."

—BENJAMIN FRANKLIN

When solving problems, create as many new ideas as possible. The more ideas you have, the more good ideas you will create. Biologists find it is easier to breed useful mutations from polypides—organisms with multiple sets of genes. There is simply more material to work with. A strong element of luck always exists when you are creating new solutions. It is easier to find a useful inspiration when you have multiple ideas with which to work. Create as many new concepts relating to your problem as you can. Every idea can be used somehow. You can even profitably use your ideas that remain unworkable throughout your lifetime because Chris Concepts have another important use.

Your ideas provide invaluable clues about the nature of your rules for solving your problem. Breaking the rules for your problem is key to

Einstein Thinking. You must identify those rules if you are going to break them. Chris Concepts are ideal for identifying your rules. We will discuss more about this in a later chapter, when we will use your new ideas to find some rules to break. So write everything down, especially the bad ideas.

IDEAS ARE GOOD (PERIOD)

"Logic is like a sword—those who appeal to it shall perish by it."

—SAMUEL BUTLER

Even if bad ideas were never recycled, they would still be worth generating. Somewhere among all those unused concepts is a solution that, when developed, will make all the errors worthwhile. Good solutions cover the cost of thousands of Chris Concepts, with plenty to spare. And, good solutions usually only come after many Chris Concepts.

Solutions have extraordinary value. The cumulative benefit just from electric lights or take-out dining is enormous. Some of the value of these innovations is returned to their creator. The rest is shared with us all. A problem solver rarely receives most of the value from a solution that has wide application, but throughout history individuals have amassed great fortunes through their innovations. But profitable solutions aren't limited just to invention. New styles of leadership, business processes, and ways of cutting costs have created tremendous value for their creators and society at large.

Don't limit your generation of ideas because you can't use most of them. Even if you don't use your Chris Concepts for an intermediate solution, as a catalyst, or even in rule breaking, generate as many ideas as you can. One of them will be brilliant, making them all worth it.

As you start the next chapter on pattern breaking, and whenever you use Einstein Thinking, remember that ideas are good. Crazy ideas, stupid ideas, ideas that can't possibly work can all move you closer to a solution to that problem. Don't let an off-the-wall Chris Concept slip away. Write it down. Learn from it. Build on it. Modify it. All your ideas are raw material for your coming solution.

CHAPTER FIVE

Breaking Patterns

> "Imagination is
> more important
> than knowledge."
>
> ALBERT EINSTEIN

Like us, Einstein grew up in a world of three dimensions. But fortunately he was not limited to just the world he knew. Einstein used his imagination to push beyond his experience into a universe of many dimensions. Although it is difficult to imagine, physicists have found that this is closer to how the universe is really structured. It can only be understood by pushing beyond what is familiar.

ESCAPING RULE RUTS

The next step in Einstein Thinking is to push beyond the rules that constrain our thinking. What we "know" is a greater obstacle than what we don't know. But clearing our minds of prejudice is as difficult as pushing all the air out of a room. Minds, like nature, abhor a vacuum. Something must displace those old rules.

Rear Admiral Grace Murray, the inventor of the computer compiler, kept a clock in her office that ran backwards. It reminded her and her guests that precedent was no reason that the status quo must continue. The clock was an excellent idea. Our biases subtly bend even conscious attempts at breaking rules back toward old thinking. We need help to get out and stay out of our rule ruts.

Seed Ideas

"When I examine myself and my methods of thought, I come to the conclusion that the gift of fantasy has meant more to me than my talent for absorbing positive knowledge."

—ALBERT EINSTEIN

Just as you can't lift yourself out of a deep physical rut without something to pull against, you need an outside idea to pull yourself out of a rule rut. We will use seed ideas to pull us beyond our rules. A seed idea provides a focus that is far away from well-worn rules about solving your problem. Thinking about your challenge in relation to the seed idea gives you a whole new perspective on possible solutions.

A good seed idea has little relation to the problem you wish to solve. It will seem ridiculous. If you wanted to end world hunger, then a nail is a good seed idea. Superficially it has nothing to do with hunger. If the relationship between the seed idea and the problem is strong, then the seed idea is inside the rule rut and can't pull you out. But an idea outside your current rules could trigger a whole series of new perspectives like "How was nail production and distribution increased a hundred fold?" "What alternatives are there to nails?" or "Could people eat nails?" If you are thinking about hunger and nails together, it is easier to consider eating bugs or genetically lowering metabolism. But without the seed idea to hold your mind open, your thinking slips right back into its old habits.

Using a seed idea will not seem serious. But you are being irrational by design. Your thinking will be sucked back to your old rules if you try to be logical. Einstein was led to his breakthrough on relativity as he imagined what it would be like to ride a beam of light—a very fanciful thought. You need equally fanciful thinking.

Adults have difficulty taking ridiculous ideas seriously. It feels stupid contemplating nails when trying to eliminate hunger. So you will probably need help selecting a useful seed idea. Otherwise, you will select a seed idea that is relevant and therefore useless. You must select seed ideas at random. It is easier to work with a stupid idea that is forced upon you, so in the next chapter we will explore some seed ideas from which you will choose through the roll of the dice. Don't sift through them until you find one that you are comfortable with. You should be uncomfortable. Pattern breaking is counterintuitive. The ridiculous is good. If a seed idea makes sense to you, then it is too close to your old way of thinking.

Idea Synthesis: Playing with the Absurd

"The point is to develop the childlike desire for recognition and to guide the child over to important fields for society."

—Albert Einstein

A seed idea alone will not give you a solution. It is only a starting place for creating useful ideas. It is a different thought, not a better thought. But as you explore the idea, play with it and find out what is interesting or insightful about it. The seed idea frees your natural brilliance to create a solution. This is idea synthesis.

Idea synthesis is like the questions Einstein asked about riding a beam of light. Would his image disappear if he looked in a mirror while riding a beam of light? It was a stupid question about an absurd idea, but it led to a brilliant solution.

Idea synthesis expands a thought into ideas that may be solutions. Because the seed idea is outside of your rut, the concepts that you wring from it will probably be outside your rut too. Idea synthesis twists, expands, and transposes ideas into clues for novel solutions. A well-crafted problem definition is vital to this process because it guides you toward a suitable answer. Once you are out of your rut, your problem statement gives you direction in your search for a solution.

I use six techniques to synthesize a good idea out of a seed idea. They are not the only ways to work with a new concept, but you can select one with a roll of a die. If you have another technique that works, use it.

Idea synthesis techniques make good habits. Habits are rule ruts, but rules have the advantage of becoming easy to use. You can use an idea synthesis habit to expand upon any new idea, helping you to see new possibilities in your ideas. Following are my idea synthesis techniques.

Humor

"The most exciting phrase to hear in science, the one that heralds new discoveries, is not 'Eureka' but 'That's funny....'"

—ISAAC ASIMOV

If you want to get serious about solving a tough problem, use humor. Any attempt at thinking about a problem in a radically new way demands a good sense of humor.

Brains have a mechanism that is the mental equivalent of an immune system—it rejects ideas that are foreign to it. Humor suppresses your mental immune system. If you treat a new idea humorously, you will be able to explore it more thoroughly because you won't immediately reject it. And your mind will be free to make other absurd connections with the seed idea, generating more concepts for solutions.

In pattern breaking, you don't want profound ideas. You want ideas that are different. Make fun of new ideas to prevent your immune system, and those of other people, from rejecting them before exploring them. Treat a new idea lightly in order to seriously consider it. This seems like a contradiction, but contradictions are key to original thinking.

Use it in a joke	Use nails to build more grocery stores with delis in areas where there is hunger.
Create a humorous picture	Eat nails.
Misuse the seed	Nail the offices of kleptocracies shut.

To get yourself in the proper frame of mind to work with a seed idea, make a joke out of it. Try forming the most ridiculous mental picture possible that associates your problem and the seed. If you can make fun of the pair at least twice, then you are probably out of your rut and ready to explore. Record your ideas as you use idea synthesis to expand on your seed idea.

Idea	Reasons Idea Will Work	Reasons Idea Won't Work
Build grocery stores	Grocery stores are part of the infrastructure needed to feed people.	The people have no money to to buy food, even if a grocery store was there.

Visualize

"The wireless telegraph is not difficult to understand. The ordinary telegraph is like a very long cat. You pull the tail in New York and it meows in Los Angeles. The wireless is the same, only without the cat."

—ALBERT EINSTEIN

We regularly see news reports of presidents and prime ministers making on-site inspections of the latest disaster. They don't actually do anything except distract busy people. Still, it isn't a bad idea, and not just because of the publicity value. The mind does a much better job of grappling with something it can see in its complete and proper context.

Mental pictures played a vital role in Einstein's thinking. He imagined problems in graphic, personal ways. Pictures allowed him to explore the implications of ideas too big or too small to actually be seen.

Make a picture of the problem you are trying to solve, or even better, three pictures. Problems are best viewed from multiple angles. These pictures can be in your head, on paper, or built with blocks. But they must be vivid images.

First, visualize the problem from its own perspective. Imagine what it looks like. How does it feel and taste? What would it like to happen? If your problem was a dispute with another division about who would have responsibility for new technology, then imagine the dispute from the point of view of the technology. You want to be developed into a solution. Who could do that best? How would you compensate the loser?

Next, think about the problem from the point of view of your seed idea. Even if the seed is a rock or a verb, imagine the point of view. This will give you a really unique perspective. Imagine your seed idea was Joan of Arc in the dispute over which division would develop the new technology. She would know that the job must be done. She would make it happen. Even if tradition dictated that it was not her responsibility, she would make certain that her team triumphed. You could do the same.

Finally, consider the seed and your problem from the viewpoint of a child. Children have brilliant human minds, but lack the complex prejudice of adult experience. Think about relationships between the seed idea and your problem that a child would notice. How would a child describe them? How would a child draw them? It may help to ask a child.

In our problem of deciding who developed a technology, a child may point out that sharing is always good. Even Joan of Arc would share. Perhaps a new interdivisional team would ensure that the technology benefited all aspects of the business.

See the problem	Bountiful, boundless earth. Powerless people.
Point of view of seed idea	Nails build the buildings, stores, and factories.
Point of view of a child	"Why don't they buy something to eat!"

After creating each picture, look for the new solutions. They may actually be a part of your mental picture. What could you add to your picture to solve the problem? What would this solution look like? Where would it come from?

Idea	Reasons Idea Will Work	Reasons Idea Won't Work
No boundaries	If bounty flowed across borders, hunger would end.	Rich and poor nations are protective of their sovereignty.
"Buy something to eat"	Hungry people could feed themselves with resources.	They have no jobs, no money.

Characteristics

"It is the theory that decides what can be observed."

—ALBERT EINSTEIN

Every seed idea has characteristics that can lead you to scores of new ideas. If your seed idea was a nail, then use the characteristics of a nail to solve your problem.

Break your seed idea down into its components. What are the parts of a nail? What are the attributes of each? How do the pieces tie together? Are the functions of the different parts unique or similar?

Break it down into similarities and differences	Builds, mass produced, simple, standard everywhere
How does it fit into its larger context?	Nails act independently with great cumulative effect. Small nails hold big things together.

Consider how the seed idea can be differentiated. How is one nail different from another? Focus on characteristics of your seed idea that shed new light on your target problem.

Idea	Reasons Idea Will Work	Reasons Idea Won't Work
Simplify foodstuffs and distribution	Food distribution is designed to satisfy the needs of wealthy nations.	People in undeveloped regions don't just want to survive, they want to prosper.

Candido Jacuzzi noticed that the pumps used for his son's hydrotherapy treatments were similar to the smaller pumps his company sold for industrial uses. With a few modifications, Jacuzzi constructed a pump that could provide hydrotherapy in the comfort of one's home. Soon he realized that the soothing jets could do more than just provide therapy, and the spa industry was born.

Applications

"People only see what they are prepared to see."

—RALPH WALDO EMERSON

Try using the seed idea as the solution. It doesn't matter how different or unconnected the problem and the seed may seem. Force the seed to be part of the answer.

This style of thinking is common when options are limited. Among the nomadic tribes that roamed the American plains, the solution was the buffalo. There were few other natural resources available. Regardless of the problem, the answer was the buffalo. How do we carry water? Make bags of buffalo stomachs. What do we eat? Eat buffalo. What do we wear? Wear buffalo skins. What do we use for cooking fuel? Burn buffalo dung. Buffaloes were used in thousands of ingenious ways because there was no choice.

When could the seed idea be the solution?	If buildings feed people.
Change the problem to fit the seed solution	Build the farms and factories needed for prosperity.
Modify the seed to be a solution	Nail becomes machinery, buildings, and roads.

By limiting your options, you force yourself to be creative outside of your normal ruts. Your seed idea is not a solution you would have suggested yourself. So you are able to explore your problem in unique, new ways. This gives you new ideas and perspectives that can evolve into a solution. You may even discover that the seed is a solution that actually works.

William Coleman stumbled across his solution seed in a rural town while working as a salesman to raise funds to complete law school. The seed was a lamp that burned brighter and better than anything on the market. Coleman made the lamp his solution. He went to work selling the lamp and made enough money to buy the rights to manufacture it. He soon had a prosperous business. When rural electrification killed the market for lamps, Coleman continued to grow his business by shifting his lamp technology to heaters. During World War II, his GI pocket stove won high praise; Ernie Pyle, a prominent American journalist at that time, ranked it just behind the jeep in usefulness. After the war, prosperity and central heating threatened Coleman's business again. But his heirs stuck with that single brilliant solution and grew the business even larger by focusing on camping equipment.

Ask yourself the following questions to spur ideas on how to use the seed idea as a solution:

Under what circumstances could it solve my problem?

How must the problem change for the seed to be a solution?

How could the seed idea be modified to be an effective solution?

Idea	Reasons Idea Will Work	Reasons Idea Won't Work
Build farms & factories	With an infrastructure of farms and factories, hungry people could feed themselves.	There is no charitable capital to build farms and factories.

Metaphors

"Without this playing with fantasy no creative work has ever yet come to birth. The debt we owe to the play of the imagination is incalculable."

—CARL JUNG

We use metaphors and similes to link different things and ideas in language. They lead us to another concept by connecting it to something

65

that we already understand. Because they connect ideas, metaphors are useful in teasing out more ideas from a seed idea. Metaphors link concepts that otherwise are dissimilar. We can use these linkages to create new patterns of thinking by linking one idea to another, and yet another until a new concept is formed. For example, portable tape players are like car stereos for the commuter on foot.

To use your seed idea as a metaphor, link it to your problem. What could tie your seed idea to your problem? It may require several intermediate links, but you can link your problem to anything. If your problem was finding a way to devote yourself full-time to composing and your seed idea was Joan of Arc, what metaphors could you create? Perhaps like Joan, you will need to put yourself in unusual and unaccustomed circumstances. Or you may need single-minded determination, like Joan. You may even go to the most important musical authority in the land and declare yourself to be the solution.

Link the situation to the seed idea	Little things like nails can have a big cumulative effect; "For want of a nail..."
What else is the seed idea like?	Nails connect to different things. Eliminating hunger requires connecting resources with hungry people.

Create more ideas from a seed by linking it to a third idea. What is the seed idea like? A paper clip is like a metal pretzel, a staple for the indecisive, the basic element of bureaucracy. Use metaphors to expand the circle of ideas you are considering by linking your seed to something else. After all, one thing leads to another, and yet another.

Idea	Reasons Idea Will Work	Reasons Idea Won't Work
Make small changes with big effects	Small changes have had enormous consequences.	Big changes are needed!

Combinations

"Everything you can imagine is real."

—Pablo Picasso

The countless different substances in our world, from goose down to granite, are made from a relatively small number of atoms combined in different ways. Atoms differ in the number of a few subatomic particles they contain. The diversity that is our universe is just electrons, protons, and neutrons mixed up in different proportions.

In the world of ideas, concepts are continually being combined to create great ideas. The first airplane was a glider with an engine. Sailboards are surfboards with sails. Giraffes are cows with long necks. Kate Gleason used the mass production techniques she learned as a supplier to Henry Ford's automobile factories to create the first subdivision of tract homes. Almost infinite variety can come from putting things together in new combinations.

Combine with old solutions	Indirect aid and nails provide subsidies to companies making capital improvements in impoverished areas.
Combine with anti-solutions	Reverse migration—move rich people to poor countries.
Combine with another seed	Nails and lily pads—make all aid (nails) contingent on successful local projects (lily pads).

Try combining your seed idea with other concepts. Start with your best conventional solutions to your problem. How could your seed idea add to those solutions? Or try to merge the seed idea with an anti-solution, a concept that seems to make your problem worse. Oxygen and hydrogen behave explosively when they are apart. Together they are benign water. You never know how characteristics may change when concepts are combined.

Combine your seed idea with a Chris Concept from your idea list. Use your toolbox of ideas to grow more ideas. Or combine one seed idea with another randomly chosen seed idea. The result is certain to be outside of your rut. For example, what ideas can you create by combining Joan of Arc with the old idea of amphibious cars? If your problem was getting a promotion, you might combine the two and realize that Joan of Arc and amphibious cars were successful in specific, unusual circumstances. What unusual circumstances would allow you to thrive and also lead to advancement? Or, if you were trying to get your spouse to join you at social functions, imagine a party where your spouse, Joan of Arc, and an amphibious car would all fit. Then remove Joan and the car.

Idea	Reasons Idea Will Work	Reasons Idea Won't Work
Reverse migration	Entrepreneurs and capitalists could make a big difference in poor countries.	Entrepreneurs and capitalists won't go to poor countries unless they can make huge profits.

No Bad Ideas

"A man of genius makes no mistakes. His errors
are volitional and are the portals of discovery."

—JAMES JOYCE

Pattern breaking exercises are successful if you break your own habits of thinking. Of course, you still want to find solutions. These ideas will all be useful. There are no bad ideas, only Chris Concepts. Even the most unlikely idea that you generate can be useful in solving a tough problem, and we will use them in the next chapter.

If you do find an idea that seems promising, record it as a solution seed. These are the ideas you feel you can grow into viable solutions. Solution seeds aren't necessarily feasible solutions, but you like them and they have potential. These are your best or most unusual ideas.

Solution Seeds
Get people from wealthy nations to move to poor nations for mutual advantage. Remove barriers to people in impoverished areas improving their own circumstances.

Idea	Reasons Idea Will Work	Reasons Idea Won't Work
Build grocery stores	Grocery stores are part of the infrastructure needed to feed people.	The people have no money to buy food, even if a grocery store was there.
No boundaries	If bounty flowed across borders, hunger would end.	Rich and poor nations are protective of their sovereignty.
"Buy something to eat"	Hungry people could feed themselves with resources.	They have no jobs, no money.
Simplify foodstuffs and distribution	Food distribution is designed to satisfy the needs of wealthy nations.	People in undeveloped regions don't just want to survive, they want to prosper.
Build farms & factories	With an infrastructure of farms and factories, hungry people could feed themselves.	There is no charitable capital to build farms and factories.
Make small changes with big effects	Small changes have had enormous consequences.	Big changes are needed!
Reverse migration	Entrepreneurs and capitalists could make a big difference in poor countries.	Entrepreneurs and capitalists won't go to poor countries unless they can make huge profits.

Figure 5.1: Idea Chart

Planting Seeds

This chapter contains a variety of seed ideas. As you can see in Figure 6.1, I organized them into six groups to help you avoid using the same type of seed idea too often. Pick your seed idea group with a roll of a die. Choose a seed idea from that group that feels uncomfortable, then return to the section on idea synthesis. Stretch your seeds.

Don't read through all of the seed ideas now. There are enough for many problems. But use a different one each time. And try coming up with even more techniques on your own.

New Territory

"The absurd is only too necessary on earth. The world stands on absurdities."

—FYODOR DOSTOYEVSKY

Any idea that is different from your old thinking can open new areas of solutions. Here are some seed ideas for moving you into new territory.

Pattern-Breaking Ideas

1. New Territory	3. New Tools	5. New Strategies
Random Nouns	Handkerchief	Poker
Ignorance Audits	Solutions	Insects
Random Verbs	Random Tools	Seven Dwarfs
Solution Surfing	Magic Feather	Monday's Child
	New Words	
2. New Solutions	Different Words	6. New Perspectives
Bigger or Smaller	New Symbols	Other Brain(s)
Answers		Hospital Bed
Sooner or Later	4. New Conditions	Generation Gap
Disasters	Parameters	Change Location
	Alternate Realities	Opposite View
	Make It Fun	

Figure 6.1: Patterns-Breaking Ideas

Random Nouns

Select one of the following nouns as your seed idea using the first three digits of your phone number or the roll of the dice.

For example, if you were looking to eliminate hunger and lived in San Francisco, your seed idea could be *paperback novels*. What could you do with a paperback novel to eliminate hunger? A tragic story of hunger could rally support in wealthy countries. An inspiring story could teach self-sufficiency in impoverished areas. These ideas are just a beginning. They can be expanded upon, breaking your pattern of thinking about the problem.

If you had a problem with a rebellious teenager and lived near Minneapolis, your seed idea could be combs. A characteristic of combs is that they straighten out tangled confusion. What issues could you straighten out with your teen, the school, or relatives? What ideas does this prompt?

Select your seed idea. Expand whatever unrelated thing you selected into some new ideas. The characteristics and metaphor idea synthesis tools work well with nouns.

Dice Roll	First Phone Digits	Topic
2	201-210	Frogs and Amphibians
3	211-300	DNA
4	301-404	First-Class Postage
5	405-419	Paperback Novels
6	420-519	No. 2 Pencils
7	520-616	King Henry VIII
8	617-708	Combs
9	709-717	Green Bananas
10	718-799	Metal Coat Hangers
11	800-816	Your Favorite Tax Form
12	817-999	Microscopes

Figure 6.2: Random Nouns

Ignorance Audits

Everyone has mental blind spots. Blind spots, or ignorance zones, are a kind of inverse rut; they are the things we don't consider because we don't understand them. Our ignorance zones are the places that we have not paid enough attention to in the past. You can increase the effectiveness of your problem statement by checking that it does not preclude ideas in your zone of ignorance.

Unfortunately, you will have a difficult time identifying your own ignorance zones. Your view of the world is centered around your sphere of competence. You are only really aware of your areas of partial ignorance. You don't even know the big holes are there. To find your zones of ignorance, you will need the help of an ignorance auditor. Find someone whose view of the world is as different from yours as possible. Look for an intelligent person with a different age, career, gender, and/or culture. Explain your problem statement to your "auditor." Then ask how your

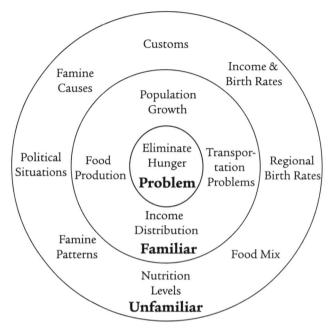

Figure 6.3: Ignorance Zones

ignorance auditor would solve the problem. Listen attentively and record his or her insights. You will probably disagree with much of it, but you need to get this viewpoint in mind as you search for solutions.

If you were trying to convince your spouse and family to move to another city, you could conduct an ignorance audit with a teenager who had recently moved. Explore the problems and opportunities the move created. Ask your auditor how he would address the problem.

Record the auditor's ideas in either the familiar or unfamiliar ring of a form like the one in Figure 6.3. If the thinking is familiar to you, record it in the inner ring. If the idea is unfamiliar, silly, or difficult to understand, record it in the outer ring. Outer ring ideas may represent whole areas of thinking that you are ignoring. Areas of ignorance are prime candidates for novel solutions. You haven't even considered them in the past, so they aren't part of your rut. Learn more about this new territory and determine if it could hold your solution.

Dice Roll	Last 2 digits of ID	Solution Verb
2	00-08	Run
3	09-19	Select
4	20-25	Advise
5	26-39	Seal
6	40-46	Atomize
7	47-57	Cede
8	58-64	Purchase
9	65-72	Withdraw
10	73-79	Contest
11	80-85	Lift
12	85-99	Congeal

Figure 6.4: Random Verbs

Random Verbs

Use a verb as a seed idea. Using the chart in Figure 6.4, select a verb with dice or the last two digits of an identification number. Then employ an idea synthesis technique to create more ideas from it.

If you were trying to find time to exercise and rolled a nine, your verb would be *withdraw*. Application idea synthesis is especially useful with verbs. How can you withdraw and have more time for exercise? Perhaps by withdrawing from other commitments. Which commitments would you select? Or, if you were lobbying for a raise and rolled a seven, how could you cede and get your raise? Perhaps conceding a contested point would get negotiations moving again. Select a verb. Use it to solve your problem.

Solution Surfing

A television is an ideal source of random ideas. With the flick of a button, you flash from one stream of consciousness to another. It is perfect for zapping yourself out of your mental rut. But your television must be used correctly. You will need a note pad, a pen, and a television with the sound turned off.

Write the words *person, place, thing,* and *action* on your pad. Then close your eyes and begin flipping channels with your remote. Stop changing channels, open your eyes, and identify the first person you see on the screen. Record the name of the person, or the type of person. Repeat the process for a place, a thing, and an action. You will have a random set of inputs. Use them to construct three or four novel solutions.

If your surfing collected a basketball player, a McDonald's, a sports sedan, and an argument, how could they resolve a disagreement with a neighbor over a tree that overhangs your property? You could put your neighbor in a sedan, drive him to a basketball game, and then settle the argument afterwards at McDonald's. You could ask that the tree be trimmed until an NBA center could stand on a sedan and not bump the branches. You could even argue that if the tree wasn't trimmed, you would be forced to sell your house to a basketball star who planned to convert it into a drive-thru McDonald's.

When your imagination is warmed up, design a viable new course of action for yourself from the items that you have written down. Break out of your rule rut!

New Solutions

*"There is always an easy solution to every human problem
—neat, plausible, and wrong."*

—H. L. Mencken

You can break your pattern of thinking about a problem by radically changing your definition of the solution. As we discussed earlier, a good definition of the real problem is vital. But what if a serious misconception of your problem is distorting your thinking? Perhaps your rules are so strong that while defining your problem, you were unable to expand your definition of a solution enough to give yourself room to maneuver. Jolt yourself out of your rule rut by dramatically altering the problem that you are trying to solve.

Bigger or Smaller Answers

Your perception of the size of your challenge may be part of the problem. You may be worrying about a mountain, when your problem is really a molehill. Test your perception by radically changing your problem's size.

What if the required solution was much bigger? Instead of finding a solution for yourself, create one for the whole world. Solve the problem for all time. Making the problem bigger does make it harder, but it also justifies a greater effort. So, if your problem is crossing a small river, think about building bridges.

Egghead Software used the bigger problem strategy in revolutionizing the competitiveness of their business. Frustrated with the difficulties of reducing costs in their many retail stores, they instead focused on a bigger, more audacious problem: how to eliminate their retail stores, selling directly to customers. And their bigger problem has had a much more satisfactory solution. Closing their stores has worked.

Or, what if your problem was really much smaller? Imagine that you only needed to solve it for a single person, or for a single hour. Smaller problems are easier to solve. Solutions that are unthinkable on a large scale are practical when applied on a small scale. As Mother Teresa said, "We cannot do great things, only small things with great love." Imagine that your advertising campaign only needed to reach one person. What would you do to influence your audience of one?

With your new problem definition, try to break through your mental barriers. Look for solutions to the now much smaller (or bigger) challenge.

Sooner or Later

Deadlines profoundly affect problems. Next month's challenge might be trivial if it were pushed back a year and your approach to next quarter's project would change if it had to be done tomorrow.

Move up the deadline for your solution to an unreasonably early date. Then consider how you would act. Panic doesn't count. Don't give up if it makes the problem impossibly hard, although giving up may be one solution. Think hard about what you would need to do. After you have developed one or more courses of action, apply them to your current deadline. What would work? What won't work?

Repeat the process with your deadline pushed far out into the future. What would be different if the solution wasn't needed for twenty years? How would your thinking change? You may find a wonderful solution that is wrong for your current deadline. Consider changing the deadline. The deadline may be the rule that makes the whole problem impossible.

If you were having difficulty merging two companies, like a Digital and a Compaq, imagine how the problem would be different if you had five years to prepare for the merger. Which divisions and products would each company have emphasized over the years to join seamlessly with the other?

Disasters

Forest fires and floods are horrible natural disasters, leaving incredible destruction in their wake. They are also very hard to stop. In the natural world, numerous species have learned to use these disasters for their own benefit. They profit instead of perishing. Pine trees take advantage of the open space that forest fires create. In a forest, living space is at a premium. Entrants have a tough time finding their own niche. Fires create new openings that a prepared pine cone can quickly fill.

Learn from their example. Perhaps a better solution target would be how to benefit from the debacle you have been working to avert. When all your hard work is leveled, think what you can do with the space. Is there room for you to expand? Since you must start over again anyway, why not improve on your original design? View the damage as a clean slate, an opportunity for you to improve on your original plans.

Young Christopher Columbus benefited when his ship was sunk battling pirates off Portugal. He almost drowned. He luckily washed ashore and found himself penniless in a foreign land. It was one of his best breaks. He had no choice but to go to Lisbon, where he married into a powerful family and became an important mariner. While in Lisbon, he also first heard the idea of going to Asia by sailing west, which also demonstrates that your best ideas may not be your own.

Floods inundate the landscape with water, but they also spread vital nutrients. For plants, the mud that is dumped everywhere is an opportunity. They take advantage of the natural fertilizer to grow and flourish. Floods in China, Mesopotamia, and Egypt nurtured the first human civilizations. Regular disaster was perfect for supporting the advance of agriculture.

When you are inundated and dumped on, consider how you can use the disaster to grow faster. Can you improve your use of time, your strategy? What is there to learn from the experience? View your flood as an opportunity to grow above your adversity. Changing your view of your disaster may not make it less of a trial, but it will make it an opportunity.

New Tools

"When the only tool you own is a hammer,
every problem begins to resemble a nail."

—ABRAHAM MASLOW

Changing the tools that you employ to solve a problem will change your thinking about it. Tools are key in shaping strategies. You have probably used some specific techniques to resolve your problem. Your dependence on these tools is hiding some other interesting solutions. Forcing yourself to use a different tool can open up scores of new solutions.

The Moslem empire swept out of Arabia using a remarkable new weapon—the tax roll. Cities opened their doors to the invaders because they knew taxes would be lowered. Taxes were equally effective in converting the new subjects to the faith. The Caliph didn't care if subjects were Moslem or not, but adherents paid lower taxes. Millions became true believers.

This section contains a number of "tools" that you should use as seed ideas. Almost anything can be a tool. For example, what if the only tool you had was a handkerchief?

Five Handkerchief Solutions

Handkerchiefs can be excellent tools for solving more than hygiene problems, if used creatively. Here are five ways to use a simple handkerchief to help reach a solution to more compelling problems.

Mask

Fold your handkerchief in half diagonally and tie it like a mask over your face. Safely disguised, do something that must get done anonymously. Important tasks are often left undone because no one wants the responsibility, or the blame. Finding a discrete way to address the problem will get things moving. If you needed to highlight some flaws in a high-profile consulting firm's strategic plan, you could do it anonymously. You may want to dispense with the handkerchief, but anonymity can give the freedom to clear obstacles.

Gag

Gag the person who has been killing your ideas. Then proceed with your solution. He cannot tell you to stop now. You may not actually use the gag, but you can still ignore the skeptic and get started. If your teenager has been complaining about a trip that will take him away from his friends, imagine that he is gagged and can't say a word. Then plan the trip. Even imaginary gags work.

Cover

Drape your handkerchief over a small object. Approach a particularly bright friend and announce that you have found the desired solution to your problem, and it is under the handkerchief. You could use this strategy if you were responsible for improving the service for an airline. Explain what the object will do, using your definition of a solution as its attributes. Ask your friend to guess what it is. He may respond with "a laptop computer power jack" or "a stiff drink." Note his answer and try to use it as a solution.

Flag of Surrender

Tie the handkerchief to a stick, and waving it over your head, meet with someone that you have been feuding with. Offer to surrender your position to get things moving and to spare the non-combatants. Ask for honorable terms but end the conflict. You could use your flag of surrender if you were striving for a particular mood in painting, but getting it wrong. Wave the surrender flag and accept the feeling you have created on canvas.

Blindfold

Cover your eyes with your handkerchief. Thus blindfolded, listen to a proposal. Ignore who is making the proposal and focus on what is being presented. Use the blindfold, whether you actually wear it or not, to remind yourself not to be prejudiced by the source of an idea. A blindfold could be the perfect tool for talking with a hostile teacher. Forget that you hate the guy and listen to what he is saying.

Random Tools

Just as a handkerchief can be used to solve serious problems, other new tools can help you break out of your rule rut. Try using one of the tools in Figure 6.5 as creatively as possible. Select the tool that corresponds to the last digit in your phone number.

Yellow Pages

Imagine that your only tools were the Yellow Pages and a telephone. The solution must be in the phone book. How would you solve your problem? If the problem were a fight with your spouse, would you call a counselor, a lawyer, or a flower shop?

Pocketknife

Pocketknives are wonderfully handy. They have been used to solve countless problems. How could you use a pocketknife to create a solution

Last Digit	New Tool
0	Yellow Pages or phone directory
1	Pocketknife
2	Press release
3	Spit and bailing wire
4	Change of heart
5	Invisibility
6	Billboard
7	Smart dog
8	Song
9	Famous aunt

Figure 6.5: Random Tools

to your problem? If you can't think of a way, you are not listening to your imagination.

A pocketknife could help you select divisional leaders in a newly acquired organization. Just pin the candidates' pictures to a corkboard. Throw the knife at the board. Select whoever the knife sticks next to. Then explain to yourself why the person was right or wrong for the job. The knife will help force decisions.

Press Release

It has been said that the pen is mightier than the sword. Imagine that your only recourse in solving your problem was to issue a two-page press release. How would you make such an opportunity into a solution? What would you say? Where would you send it? What actions would you want your readers to take?

Imagine that you needed a baby-sitter so that you could go to the theater. What would your press release say to assure yourself of an eager, competent sitter? Now use what you learned from your release to get the baby-sitter.

Spit and Bailing Wire

Fixing things with only spit and bailing wire has become a cultural cliché. But if that was all you had, how would you employ it to solve your target problem?

If your problem was raising money for a new CAT scan machine at the hospital, you could construct a CAT scan machine with bailing wire and an Etch A Sketch in the lobby. Remind patrons that only their donations can replace the bailing wire version with a real community asset.

Change of Heart

What kind of solution would you pursue if you could cause a change of heart in a single person? Whom would you select? How would you modify his or her opinion? Now go convince that person!

A change of heart can work for all kinds of problems. Even if you are developing a new vaccine for the flu, there is someone who could speed your work. Perhaps it is someone with a special skill or who controls a useful facility. Identify this person. How would you cause a change of heart to get the help you need?

Invisibility

As far as I know, there is no way for you to be physically invisible. But if you could be invisible at will, how could you use invisibility to solve your problem?

Perhaps you want to write a passionate love song. Where would you invisibly slip to get the material for your song? What kinds of emotions would you look for? Imagine what you would find, then use it for your song.

Billboard

What if the only tool at your disposal was a large billboard on which you could display any message you wished? What would you say? Where would you place it?

If you were raising seed capital for a new venture, you may put the three main bullet points of your business plan on the billboard, along with your phone number. Even if you don't use the billboard, use the concise message you develop.

Smart Dog

Can you devise a solution to your problem if your only tool was a dog? Of course it must be a smart dog, like Lassie, so it can do whatever you wish that is within a dog's power. But your only course of action is something the dog can do. What would you have it do? How would you solve the problem with a dumb dog?

Imagine you wanted a date with someone in your building. What could the dog carry to him/her that would start the right conversation? How could you do the same thing without the dog?

Song

What if a song was your solution? Imagine that you can write one really great song. Everyone will hear it and love it. What message would you write into that song to help solve your target problem?

Perhaps your song needs to smooth a difficult group reorganization. What tune would win you the support you need—"Fifty Ways to Leave Your Lover" or "Happy Days Are Here Again"? How should it make your team members feel? The refrain will carry the key message you want everyone to remember. Now deliver the message without the song.

Famous Aunt

How would you solve your problem if your only tool was a famous aunt? Everyone who is anyone knows and loves her. She is very fond of you, but won't give you money lest it spoil you.

How would you solve a problem using a famous aunt? One way is to use your well-connected aunt to introduce you to someone who can help you directly. Who is that person for you? Now determine how you are going to get together with this person without the help of a famous aunt.

Magic Feathers

Magic feathers are an interesting tool. Although they change the reality of a situation very little, their impact can be enormous. Dumbo, the little elephant with the big ears, was able to fly after some helpful crows gave him a "magic" feather to help him off the ground. While the feather did nothing to improve Dumbo's ability to fly, it did give his confidence a big boost. Believing that he could fly, he did.

Tough problems need magic feathers. It is difficult to do anything unless you first believe that it can be done. You will not try hard enough or long enough until you are convinced that you can succeed.

Magic feathers can be anything that imparts confidence. It might be a diploma or a platinum card. A public endorsement of your abilities or a private memory of a past triumph both work well. What would give you the extra confidence you need to do the impossible? A friend's business made dramatic advances after he acquired a tailored suit, an office, and expensive name cards. He felt like a player, and soon was.

To discover what could work as a magic feather for you, think of someone that has had the success you are seeking. This person will be your model. Write this person's name on the top of a sheet of paper. Then list as many of the person's positive attributes, both tangible and intangible, as you can. You might list that your model is patient or that she drives a red convertible.

Review the list, and pick out an attribute that would make you feel more like your model. It should also be something you would very much like to acquire or develop. Buy it, foster it, or fake it—whatever it takes. Just getting your magic feather will help to boost your confidence and effectiveness.

New Words

The words that describe your solution may not exist yet. If they don't, you will be misled by vocabulary that describes some other situation. Use new words to describe the new idea you will create.

To invent your new idea vocabulary, substitute words of your own creation for the more general terms that you have used to describe your opportunity or problem. Include a word that represents your desired solution. These words are placeholders for the ideas that you will have.

Physicists regularly invent particles, like quarks, to solve problems. Quarks filled a need before there was any evidence of their existence. Then, after the solution was defined, the quarks were found.

Use new words in talking and thinking about your challenge. As you use your new words to describe your solution, you will discover their meaning. New words are free to mold themselves to fit your solution—they have no other definitions to distract you.

For example, if you needed to develop a menu item to compete with a competitor's pizza, you could call the item Zalt. If you called it the Super Taco project instead, your mind would be 99 percent made up. Explain to a colleague what Zalt is, how much it costs, how it tastes, and how to prepare it. Discover what is needed to solve your problem.

If you like, use any of the words that follow as the basis of your new vocabulary.

Shure	Kado	Mata
Sugu	Bilup	Desi
Hara	Gramal	Feng
Jer	Thrax	Zalt

Different Words

Words like typhoon, crusade, or plague can add powerful images and emotions to ideas that you are only beginning to develop. Try applying them to your problem. Any word that is not normally used in conjunction with your problem can be used.

Take a phrase like *market share loss* that you use repeatedly in discussing your problem. Replace it with stronger nouns and verbs that are unrelated to the problem, words like pandemic or meltdown. Observe how saying "meltdown" changes your thinking about the severity of the problem.

New Symbols

Einstein used the powerful symbolic language of mathematics to solve his problems. The same strategy can work for us, particularly for problems that we don't consider mathematical. Inventing symbols for a problem provides a useful, new point of view. It may be just the thing to get you out of your rule rut.

If you were concerned about your child's friends, you could assign symbols to all the children in your area. Then write equations showing who gets along and who doesn't. Look for a solution by manipulating the equations. Perhaps you have never thought of $s + e - b$ before.

Create symbols to represent elements of your problem. Represent the people involved, the physical circumstances, or the emotions. Create new, unique operations that allow the symbols to interact. Go beyond plus and minus. Playfully manipulate the symbols to describe your problem and search for a solution. You are not trying to create a new branch of mathematics. Use symbols to probe your own view of the problem.

Do your calculations inspire any new insights? How would you solve your problem symbolically? What missing variables are needed to make it work? Express a useful solution. Force yourself to look at the problem in a new way.

NEW CONDITIONS

"Necessity, who is the mother of invention."

—PLATO

Conditions surrounding a problem are an essential part of the problem. These conditions include key parameters, roles, and attitudes. Changing them alters your perception of problems and solutions, and may help you to break your rules. Spain was the preeminent naval power of the sixteenth century. Her numerous fleets of large ships made her unbeatable. But conditions were changing. Small, fast sailing designs and longer range cannons were making the Spanish fleet obsolete. A few English captains realized this. By thinking with these new parameters in mind, they tipped the scales of naval power in England's favor, and it remained that way for three centuries.

Parameters

Problems have parameters—the facts behind key assumptions. We like to think of parameters as constants, but they often change dramatically. When they change, the set of possible solutions changes with them. Heavier-than-air flight may have been impossible in 1803. But by 1903, parameters had changed. Light-weight engines of sufficient power were available. Fuel efficiency had increased. There were better materials and better tools. Flight was a viable solution. Now parameters are changing faster than ever before.

Imagine how it would change your problem if one of the key parameters was to change dramatically. Select a parameter of your problem and randomly change it in one of the ways listed in Figure 6.6. Use the direction of your commute or a roll of the dice to select your change. If you roll a one or commute north, double the price of a key parameter of your problem.

Visualize your problem in a world where the parameters had changed. Would there still be a problem? Would you still try to find a solution? How would your approach to a solution change? What new solutions would be available to you? Use this changed reality to explore new ideas that have seemed impractical in the past.

Double the Price

Prices are an important part of most problems. Imagine that a key price for your problem was doubled. It happens quite often. Double your taxes, double your income, double labor costs. Then try to think of a novel solution that fits the new conditions. For example, every time petroleum prices have gone up, new oil fields have become viable. Arctic oil and deep sea drilling are profitable solutions because the prices went up.

Dice Roll	Typical commute direction	Parametere Change
1	North	Double the Price
2	South	Make It Free
3	Up	Ten Times the Reward
4	East	Change Sides
5	West	No Punishment
6	Down	Remove a Hassle

Figure 6.6: Parameters

Make It Free

Instead of doubling the price, make your parameter free. Free is a useful approximation of an insignificant cost. A surprising number of costs have become insignificant. Computer costs and telecommunications charges have fallen to levels that would have been considered almost free twenty years ago. What would happen if your parameter became practically free? How could you make that happen?

Ten Times the Reward

Rewards are important conditions in any situation. As part of your problem definition, you specified carrots that you can expect for solving the problem. Imagine that your reward has been increased tenfold. If you needed to increase sales in your region by 25 percent, could you succeed if your reward was to retire in luxury at the end of the year? Options that you once dismissed suddenly become possible. So increase the reward for your solution, and see what solutions it creates.

Change Sides

Imagine that everything about your current situation is the same, only now you are on the other side. You have your competitor's strengths and weaknesses. You are working to beat yourself. Consider your situation in these new circumstances. What would you do?

If your problem was to prevent a rival telephone company from entering your market, imagine how you would break into your turf. Which strategy would you adopt? What first steps would you take? Then go and counter those strategies.

No Punishment

Penalties and the fear of failure are key conditions in any situation. They preclude a number of actions, and often rightly so. However, these punishments should not be obstacles to your thinking. So imagine that there are no penalties. Anything goes. How would you solve your problem?

If your problem was to develop a new artistic style, imagine that there would be no criticism of your experimental attempts. Your friends wouldn't laugh. Your galleries wouldn't have second thoughts about you. There are no repercussions. How would this change what you were willing to try?

Remove a Hassle

Often something that is only peripheral to a problem, like onerous paperwork or getting consensus, is enough to tip the balance against a solution. But if that hassle were eliminated, how would you create a solution?

If you were looking for a cure for cancer, imagine there were no regulatory or financial restraints. You could pursue any course you believe is best. What would you do? Why is it different from what you are doing? How could you pursue this strategy with the existing constraints?

Alternate Realities

Instead of changing the basic details of the problem you are trying to solve, change the rest of the world. Imagine solving your problem in a totally different environment. Move your problem to another century, and you have a whole new challenge to stimulate your creativity. Or map the entire situation surrounding your problem statement into a movie plot or comic book. The circumstances and options will change dramatically, but the core issues remain the same. It may be easier to see a solution in this altered reality.

To alter the reality of your problem, choose a situation. You can select one from the list in Figure 6.7 with a roll of the dice or using the time you woke up last Saturday. For example, if you rolled a six or arose at 7:30 A.M., transfer your problem to Cleopatra's Egypt. You are Cleopatra. If your problem was arranging the time and the money for a European vacation, then the vacation could be undisputed mastery of the eastern Mediterranean, your boss could play the part of Caesar, and your spouse could be Mark Anthony. How would Cleopatra solve this problem? What can you apply from her solution?

If you didn't go to sleep last Friday night because you were preparing for a hearing on a contested zoning change or rolled a two, imagine that you and your opponents are going to have a food fight instead. How will you win? Should you escalate or hang back? Will it be cream pies or dinner rolls? What can you learn from your food fight strategy to prepare for the hearing?

Select a scenario and see if an alternate reality helps solve your problem.

Dice Roll	Hour You Arose Last Saturday	Alternate Reality
2	Didn't go to sleep	A Food Fight
3	Earlier than 4 A.M.	Romeo & Juliet
4	4 to 6 A.M.	First Century Rome
5	6 to 7 A.M.	Star Wars
6	7 to 8 A.M.	Cleopatra
7	8 to 9 A.M.	Joan of Arc
8	9 to 10 A.M.	Eighteenth Century France
9	10 A.M. to 12 P.M.	Snow White
10	Noon or later	1968 in Your Hometown
11	Don't know	Seventeenth Century Japan
12	Never know	A Kindergarten Class

Figure 6.7: Alternate Realities

Make It Fun

Everyone hates to do something, and those tasks are unlikely to get done. Perhaps some attitudes need to change to make a solution to your problem possible. Fun things happen. Here are some ways to make a solution more fun.

Work/Party

The work/party or "barn raising" strategy is a time-honored way to make work fun. If you want to develop a new mutual fund product, then invite some friends over and make it into a party. Refreshments and music are usually enough, although you could give away T-shirts or provide war paint. Explain that the party is to unleash everyone's creative ideas for a distinctive mutual fund. Collect ideas on posters around the room. As the party progresses, have an "idea pageant" and vote on the most original idea.

Organize the task so that it can be completed in one party. It will be harder to get original ideas at a follow-up party. Work through some of the initial obstacles to your ideas too. Attack the obvious issues to your mutual fund concepts during the party. It will be much easier to work through objections while everyone is happy and uninhibited.

Tangible Reward

Purchase something that you've always wanted, gift wrap it, and have a friend hold it for you until you finish the task. If your problem is trying to find a compelling rationale for a grant proposal, and you are also a tennis fanatic, then buy your dream racket for yourself. Give it to a friend, preferably another tennis player. As an added incentive, tell her that she can keep the gift if you don't finish your proposal by the deadline. Then find that compelling rationale, and get your racket.

Contest

Competition makes everything more interesting. People do crazy things when they compete. They spend months in pain, risk their lives, and spend huge sums of money in order to win. So harness that competitive drive. Challenge a friend to a contest involving your problem. See who can finish faster, better, or in more style.

If your problem was to launch a new product, find a friend who also has a product to launch. Wager that your product will ship earlier relative to its target launch date than your friend's product will ship relative to its launch date. You can even bring colleagues and family into the rivalry. Call your friend regularly to check on his progress and inspire yourself to try harder. Motivation is key to creative solutions. Give yourself lots of motivation.

Or, compete against yourself by inventing a game. Award yourself points for progress; for example you could get points for each blank you fill in on your tax form. Create the potential for failure too by taking away points for mistakes. Then play to win!

Record the Triumph

Use a camera or video camera to record your triumph. Since you are recording your struggle for posterity, put on a good show. If your target problem is to get a child to complete his homework, then take his picture holding each completed assignment like a trophy fish. Post the pictures. Send them to grandparents. Recording a triumph makes it sweeter and lengthens your child's memory of success.

Buy the Trophy

Buy yourself a big trophy or plaque to memorialize your triumph. For example, if you are trying to win a coveted job, have a trophy made memorializing your advancement. Get the trophy first, before you get the job. This gives you a powerful incentive. You will look very foolish if you don't succeed. You will do almost anything for the trophy and the job.

Find an Audience

Find an audience that will cheer you on to victory. Give yourself the home team advantage. If you are trying to finish your taxes, recruit family or friends for moral support. Have them check on your progress every hour. When you make headway, you deserve their accolades. When you finish, do a victory lap around the house. You will find it impossible to procrastinate in front of your fans. Besides, they may even help.

Location, Location, Location

Pick a good location for solving your problem. The organizers of dull conventions understand this motivation well. That's why there are so many meetings in Hawaii. You (and your helpers) will get excited about a job if you can go somewhere fun to do it. If your problem is pulling together a critical brief with several colleagues, check into a downtown hotel. Hammer out the brief with the promise of a night on the town as soon as it is done. For a bigger problem, try a sabbatical week at a resort. Make your location part of your motivation.

Make the Job Desirable

Tom Sawyer got his friends to paint the fence—and pay for the privilege—by making it desirable. How can you make your problem interesting enough that someone would want to help you with the solution? One of the best ways to accomplish this is to give your problem solver free reign to create a solution. If your problem is to find an exciting new packaging concept, offer the job to a class of design students without restrictions. Encourage them to break the rules. The freedom to create is a powerful motivation. Use it to get the help you need.

NEW STRATEGIES

"One tries to make plans fit the circumstances."

—GEORGE PATTON

Some strategies are so tightly entwined with a problem that it seems impossible to separate them. The strategy may be the problem. Consider a very new strategy selected at random. See if it will work for your problem. Here are a number of different exercises for changing strategies.

Poker

Good poker strategies have application beyond card games. Draw a card from a handy deck, or just visualize one. After you have a card, select a new strategy based on the card's suit—hearts, spades, diamonds, or clubs.

Hearts

It is time for you to bluff. Determine what would be required for you to be in a position of strength. Make a list. Then act as though you had everything on the list. Deal with others from your position of strength.

If your problem was getting your kids to eat a healthier diet, determine what would give you a position of unassailable strength. Perhaps if the house were devoid of junk food and your children were broke, they would have to eat healthy food. Discuss the problem with your children, employing the option. While you are bluffing, be sure to work on realizing the items on your list. Get rid of the junk food because you can't bluff forever.

Spades

You need to raise the ante to find a solution. Increase your own commitment to success. If you have only a small stake in the outcome, you won't try hard enough. Create some new incentives that make a solution even more vital. Boasts or wagers can be powerful personal motivators. If your problem is to seamlessly electronically link two offices, publicize your completion date. Bet your boss that you will finish on time. Even better, increase the incentives for everyone that you are working with. Arrange for a team bonus if you hit the target date. Make winning essential to you and your team.

Diamonds

You should fold. Admit to yourself that while you probably could win if you threw enough energy and wealth at the problem, the victory would not be worth the cost. Remember that you will get most of your satisfaction out of a small percentage of your activities. Fold the losers and put your time and energy into winning hands.

If your problem is to increase sales of a line of frozen dinners by 50 percent so that the line would break even, folding could be the right solution. End the product line and put your energy and money somewhere else. There are many problems that aren't worth solving. See if yours is one of them.

Clubs

It is time to draw some new cards for your hand. Decide which of the skills, strategies, or plans that you are holding should be discarded, and replace them. If your situation is bad, get rid of at least half. It will not be easy to lay aside the familiar for the unknown or unproven, but the odds favor a change. Go for it.

If you are trying to increase the reimbursement levels your dental practice receives from the health plans you are affiliated with, consider drawing some new cards. Cancel with the health plans that pay too little. You will not turn them into a winning hand. Focus your energies on rebuilding your client base from plans with reasonable compensation for services.

Insects

Insects have many unique perspectives on solving problems. Not only are many of their strategies different from human strategies, but there are dramatic differences between species. Borrow one. Imitate the strategy of the last insect you saw.

Fly

Do you remember the last fly you watched? It buzzed about in wild, random patterns. It got around, moving fast and covering lots of territory until it found something interesting. Then it swooped, again and again. If you shooed it away, it just made a big circle and came back.

Think and act like a fly. Try to randomize your search for new opportunities to exploit. Give the broader world a buzz. Move quickly, investigating anything that may be interesting. Get around obstacles by trying many angles of attack. Don't give up too easily. Take your investigation far outside your usual turf. The worst thing that can happen is that you will gain a greater appreciation of where you are now.

If the last insect you saw was a fly and your problem is closing a difficult acquisition arrangement, what fly-like strategies could you adopt? Perhaps you could rapidly appraise a number of alternate deals. Determine what you would do if the current deal fell through. And even if you came back to the original candidate, your explorations will have yielded valuable ideas about the acquisition's value and strategy.

Spider

Most spiders are very different from flies. They construct webs to ensnare the next meal that blunders by. The webs are carefully placed, carefully constructed. Then, with their preparations complete, spiders wait.

Try thinking like a spider. Anticipate the opportunities that will come to you. Carefully prepare yourself so that when the great chance swoops by, you can latch on, secure it, and profit from it. Think where you should be. Set your net. Tell the right people about your interests. Have friends watch for your opportunity. Be ready to move decisively. Preparation creates opportunity. A current résumé, a ready source of funding, or the right equipment could prevent your opportunity from getting away.

If your problem is still a difficult acquisition, but the last insect you saw was a spider, then consider how you could be better prepared to execute an acquisition next time around. Improve your financial resources. Assign key players to a readiness team. Reach consensus within your organization on candidates and strategies. Now that you are better prepared, you just have to wait for your opportunity. You may even find that this time around you will snare your original target.

Ant

By itself, the ant is not a formidable creature. But ants don't hang around by themselves. They live in large and powerful groups. Ants make their presence felt through sheer numbers, even clear-cutting plots of rain forest.

Think like an ant. You aren't going to do it all by yourself. You need an army of helpers striving toward your goal. Consider how achieving your goals will benefit others. People in your organization, profession, neighborhood, or family want many of the same things that you do. You should be working together.

Make a list of the people or groups that would profit from you reaching your objectives. Determine how you will motivate them to help.

Imagine you still need to complete that difficult acquisition, but the last insect you saw was an ant. Thinking like an ant, you would get outside help with the acquisition. Who would want the parts of the target company that you don't need? Who inside the target company could be on your side? Line up others that could benefit from the deal to help make it happen.

Seven Dwarfs

The seven dwarfs, the little guys that ran around with Snow White, each had their own personal strategy for life. Here are seven problem-solving strategies, one for each dwarf. Use the strategy corresponding to your favorite dwarf or the dwarf most like your boss. Decide upon a dwarf before you read the strategies, or you will select a dwarf who doesn't break your rules.

To illustrate how each dwarf could provide a successful strategy, imagine that you have a horrible, nerve-wracking commute. It is sapping your most productive time and draining away your energy. Your top priority is fixing this commute.

Sneezy

It is hard to solve a problem if you keep everything inside. Vent your frustrations. Get it out of your system and onto the table. Begin with a tape recorder and/or a sympathetic listener. Talk the problem through. Getting emotional or passionate can't hurt. In fact, you must be passionate if you are really going to bring everything out. Afterwards, you may want to take notes of what you said. Group the facts, your predictions and your emotions on another sheet of paper. Construct a course of action that fits your list.

If you were using a "Sneezy" strategy to solve your commute problem, you would start by venting your frustrations to some of the key people involved, such as your boss and your spouse. They might not have understood the extent of the problem. But more importantly, as you verbalize your issues it will become apparent what bothers you most about your commute and what a potential solution needs to include. Whether it is working different hours to avoid rush-hour traffic, moving, finding a new job, or working from home, there is a solution that meets your needs. After the problem is clear, you can make the solution happen.

Happy

Few people accomplish things they really didn't believe they could do. But almost anyone can achieve what he believes will be done. Be optimistic. Focus on convincing yourself that you can do it, and you will.

One "Happy" strategy for the commute problem is to make your time in the car or on the train as enjoyable as possible. Use the time to listen to your favorite books or learn a foreign language. Prepare for each trip. You might enjoy the trip more if you took a few extra minutes and drove calmly and sedately, or if you aggressively worked at shortening your time. Pursue the strategy that makes you the happiest.

Sleepy

Your intractable problem will seem much more manageable after some rest and relaxation. Sleep on the problem. Have some fun. Give your unconscious mind some time to work things out. Restore your personal energy. Just because you are relaxing doesn't mean your mind isn't still hard at work.

A "Sleepy" strategy for working through the commute problem would be to take a few days off and avoid your commute altogether. Show yourself exactly what you are missing by enduring that miserable commute every day. When you are thoroughly rested and relaxed, ask yourself if that commute is worth it. If it isn't, change it. If it is, make the best of the situation you have chosen.

Dopey

Ignorance isn't always such a bad thing. If you don't know something is impossible, you may succeed in doing it. Dopey would have tried the hardest to do the impossible. Pretend that the impossible is achievable. Work on your problem as though the major obstacles don't exist.

Using a "Dopey" strategy on the commute problem, you could be blissfully ignorant of the hours you are required to keep. Simply come and go to work when traffic is light. Reduce your hours to compensate for your drive. Don't protest that this isn't allowed. You don't know any better.

Doc

No one knows everything. Get some learned advice. Ask an expert. Articulating your situation to someone else will help you to better understand your problem. It is not necessary that they understand your particular problem, only that they know a thing or two.

An expert who could give appropriate advice for the commute problem may be someone who has rearranged her life to eliminate her commute. Find out how she did it, and if it was worth it.

Grumpy

Pessimistic solutions are very robust. Pessimists think about everything that could go wrong. Glib assurances are not enough for them. Think like Grumpy. Consider what else could go wrong in your current scenario. How would you deal with the added difficulties? How can you minimize the chance of disaster?

A grumpy problem solver with a bad commute would humph that he was certain to be laid off anyway, so he might as well quit now and find a job closer to home. Or he would despair of finding a career closer to home and move near work. Either way, he reduces the pain of those inevitable breakdowns and traffic jams.

Bashful

You need a shy solution that requires only you. Don't wait for others to make a decision or take action. Your solution may never even be one of their priorities. Determine how you can solve the problem on your own authority, and your own initiative.

A shy solution to your commute problem would be to strike out on your own working from home. Your family need not move. No one can complain about your hours. You simply do it, and end your commuting misery.

Monday's Child

Monday's child is fair of face,
Tuesday's child is full of grace,
Wednesday's child is full of woe,
Thursday's child has far to go,
Friday's child is loving and giving,
Saturday's child works hard for a living,
But the child that's born on the Sabbath day, is bonny and blithe, and good and gay.

Since everyone was born on one of seven days of the week, the day of your birth is a good random solution strategy. Use the day of your birthday this year if you can't remember on which day of the week you were born.

Monday

Pay more attention to playing your part. Does your language and tone of voice fit with your role? Are you dressing the part? How do you act? Dress, talk, and act like the person who will solve the problem.

Tuesday

Look for a more graceful, subtle solution. Consider ways to get the same effect with less effort. Think about simple, comprehensive remedies.

Wednesday

Turn your full attention and energy on that problem which has caused you so much grief. You have suffered enough woe. Put other projects on hold until you have found a solution.

Thursday

Focus on a long-term solution to your problem. Don't be led from your path by short-term fixes. Concentrate your time and talents on long-term success.

Friday

Show more affection for those you love, and appreciation for those that help you. If you love someone, tell him today and tomorrow too. If you should be grateful to someone, thank her. Make it clear why you are grateful. This may not solve your problems, but they will seem much smaller.

Saturday

Solve your problem with a liberal measure of hard work. Roll up your sleeves and persevere until you succeed.

Sunday

You need to accentuate the positive in your life. Focus on how to best enjoy your present circumstances. You will find a solution to your problem in the near future, but think about how to "smell the roses" today.

NEW PERSPECTIVES

"Physical concepts are free creations of the human mind, and are not, however it may seem, uniquely determined by the external world."

—ALBERT EINSTEIN

Everyone has very different views of reality. Each viewpoint highlights, or obscures, a different set of ideas. Changing your perspective can make solutions pop out from obscurity. All you must do is change your point of view.

Ask the Other Brain

Could the answers you've been seeking be on the other side of your head? Your brain is really two brains. You use one of them more, but the other brain is just as clever in a different way. It too has been diligently gathering information on your problem, and may have a solution for you.

However, because of your dominant brain, the other brain has had trouble making its opinions known. Give your other brain an avenue to expresses its ideas.

To divine a solution from your other brain, switch hands and techniques. If you are right-handed, use your left hand. If you are left-handed, use your right. If you use words to examine problems, switch to pictures. Use words if you think visually. For variety, you may also use different drawing or writing instruments such as crayons or paintbrushes instead of a pen.

With your other hand and the new medium, describe your problem. Include important details, peripheral facts, or even random nonsense. As you describe the problem, possible solutions will start popping out. Capture them in the style you are using to describe your problem. Be careful not to revert to your usual style, whether it is words or pictures. Your dominant brain will probably get excited over a new idea, and want to take over. Don't let it! It will get its chance later. When you decide you are done, you will have a unique description of your problem and some good solutions from a knowledgeable insider.

Switching to the left or right brain isn't your only option for changing your mind's perspective. Some portions of your brain are more emotional while others are more objective.

If you have been trying to solve your problem objectively, you might have a completely different perspective if you become emotional about it instead. Get angry or excited. Use the emotional centers of your brain.

If thinking about your problem makes you highly emotional, calm down. Consider solutions from a detached viewpoint. Imagine that it is someone else's problem—you will not be affected by the outcome and are only giving dispassionate advice. Let the more rational portions of your brain work on the challenge.

Hospital Bed

Limitations can force you to be more creative about solutions. Imagine that you have been hospitalized. Your condition is serious and your activity is sharply limited. You are only allowed one visitor and two phone calls before you will be sedated until tomorrow, when you will be allowed another visitor and two brief telephone calls.

Imagine that your problem is managing offices in Tokyo, London, and New York. It is diverting all of your energy from other responsibilities. If you were stuck in a hospital bed, your strategy for solving the problem must change. How would you succeed? Perhaps you would delegate key responsibilities to staff members in each office and set up mandatory conference calls to coordinate their activities. Or you may restructure operations so that each office works autonomously and coordination is minimal. Either way, you could run things from a hospital room, or find the time for your other responsibilities.

Generation Gaps

Different generations have very different ways of viewing things. The thought process of a twelve-year-old differs from the ninety-two-year-old. If you got up on the left side of the bed this morning, try to find a solution as though you were twelve years old. Twelve-year-olds have answers to almost every problem, except perhaps how to keep a room clean. Twelve-year-olds are masters of ad hoc, thrown-together solutions. They can fix anything, given enough tape and string. They can do anything. They have boundless energy too. Create a twelve-year-old solution.

If your problem is staffing a growing business in a tight labor market, you could decide to make your office the most fun place to work in the city. Have video games and toys, pizza parties, and ski trips. It would be such a great place to work that you would be swamped with energetic applicants.

If you got up on the right side of the bed, then imagine finding your solution as a ninety-two-year-old. You keenly understand the value of both the present and your own legacy. You have a clear idea of just how important your solution will be fifty years from now. Create a ninety-two-year-old solution.

A ninety-two-year-old solution to the staffing problem may be to provide workers with security and respect. You would give your employees responsibility and authority for their work, and the security of knowing you would stand by them even when they made mistakes. Employees stay with you, and bring in their friends for the stable, satisfying environment.

Change Location

Familiar environments reinforce familiar thoughts. If you stay around the same people and the same places, you are likely to think the same thoughts. But when you change environments, it becomes easier to imagine new concepts. Isaac Newton had some of his greatest insights after the plague forced him to flee Cambridge for his home in Lincolnshire. The change of place was liberating.

There are many ways to get away. Leaving town is one. You could also work on your problem in a café, library, or park. Or, you and a friend could cruise a freeway or a back road while you talk through ideas. Each environment will stimulate slightly different ideas.

You can change your environment by hanging around with a different crowd. Investment bankers and performance artists or school teachers and accountants can give each other valuable new perspectives.

If your problem was enforcing a curfew with a rebellious teenager, then go to the park for the afternoon. Get away from the tension at home. Change your location, watch some children play, and see what ideas the change of scenery liberates.

The Opposite View

You can readily gain a new perspective by adopting the opposite view on issues relating to your problem. Recast the facts. Change your opinion. As you take the other side, note the change in your thinking. After you create an opposite solution, reverse it again. See what ideas it gives you for a real solution.

If your problem was finding a way to promote a brilliant junior member of the team without alienating capable veterans, take the opposite view. How would you promote a veteran and still keep the brilliant new-comer? Perhaps you would assign her to create a high-profile strategic plan or lead an upcoming negotiation. Now apply that solution to your capable veterans.

CHAPTER SEVEN

Breaking Rules

> "So far as the laws of
> mathematics refer to
> reality, they are not
> certain. And so far as
> they are certain, they
> do not refer to reality."
>
> —ALBERT EINSTEIN

Einstein was a consummate rule breaker. He grew up hating senseless regulations. Flagrantly or slyly, he broke every rule he despised. He got into repeated trouble at school, although he was a brilliant student. He did not get a university post until he was one of the world's leading scientists because he resisted academic protocols. He renounced his German citizenship and became stateless. His constant battle with the rules caused Einstein much personal difficulty, but it had a positive influence on his scientific research. He had no trouble breaking the rules that blinded his contemporaries to important ideas. Einstein's musings on physical phenomena while riding on a beam of light led him to identify, and break, the key rule that had kept other physicists from relativity. Einstein realized that time need not be absolute. By violating this inviolable rule, Einstein solved one of science's most important problems. Appendix B shows how breaking this one rule led to the first of a series of amazing solutions. Learning to think like Einstein is learning to break the rules.

You've Got to Break the Rules

"Particularly pleasing was the possibility that Joshua might be so stuck on his classical way of thinking that I would accomplish the unbelievable feat of beating him to the correct interpretation of his own experiment."

—James Watson

Every problem has a solution, but some tasks can't be done. We make solutions unattainable by making these impossible tasks a condition of the solution. Bureaucracies are particularly adept at making the simplest activities unrealizable. If a problem seems to defy any solution, a rule is at the heart of the difficulty. You can't both follow convention and solve a tough problem. You must break the rules.

Legend says that Alexander the Great solved an early impossible problem, the Gordian knot. It was an incredibly complex knot joining two ropes. Whoever had the wisdom and skill to resolve the Gordian knot would become ruler of all Asia. Alexander sliced it neatly in two with his sword. He then conquered Asia with similar directness.

Some may object that Alexander was not a true rule breaker. It was not a "real" rule that one couldn't cut the knot. Everyone had just assumed that the knot must be untied. But this is true of most rules. Rules are only unbreakable if we assume they are so.

Rules do serve a useful purpose. We should respect them when it is moral and prudent to do so. But rules are not truth. They are a convenient shorthand for truth. There are times when even cherished rules must be broken. However, our respect for rules is so great that we just can't do that. Rules are too vital to our understanding of the world. Instead, we look for ways to prop up the very misconceptions that are keeping us from a solution.

Early astronomers had an "everything revolves around the earth" rule. It worked well. Only planets didn't fit the rule perfectly. But instead of discarding the rule because it didn't work some of the time, astronomers invented additional rules to explain the wandering of planets. The complicated rules predicted a planet's motion with amazing accuracy. It was a brilliant effort, but all wrong. And the partial success of those rules stifled further progress.

Logical, well-reasoned rules prevent solutions. One city found that it could reduce car/pedestrian accidents by removing crosswalks, a clear violation of the "crosswalks equals safety" rule. Making pedestrians wary as they crossed the street turned out to be more effective than creating an artificial zone of safety. But it was a hard rule to break.

Successful businesses have a tough time breaking the rules that made them successful in the first place. The rules have worked so well. The business is organized around those rules. This repeatedly leaves them vulnerable to competitors who are willing to challenge the old rules. How could a time-tested rule be an impediment to a solution? Rules mislead in many ways. Here are just a few.

Things Change

"Truths are illusions of which one has forgotten that they are illusions."

—FRIEDRICH NIETZCHE

We think of our current solutions as the pinnacle of human achievement; after all, no one has done better yet. But any endeavor from athletics to zoology will be improved upon. There will not just be small changes but enormous, major advances.

In 1904, the year before Einstein published his three remarkable papers that changed the world, it was hard to imagine how the world could change significantly. They had democracy, although most of the population was disenfranchised. Athletes were closing in on the absolute limits of human performance. Ships, telephones, and even airplanes had already been invented. It seemed as if nothing could possibly change much.

As Figure 7.1 illustrates, the rules have changed since 1904. They will change again, dramatically. But the here and now feels so permanent that it is hard to imagine what those changes will be.

	1904	1996	2086
High Jump	5' 11"	8' ½"	10' 9¼"
New York to Paris	6 days	2.5 hours	18 minutes
100 Meter dash	11.0 seconds	9.86 seconds	8.9 seconds
Pole Vault	11' 5 ¾"	20' 1½"	28' 3"
100-Meter Freestyle	62.8 seconds	48.42 seconds	38.37 seconds
Discus	136'	243'	310'
Voting Franchise	White males 21 years and older	18 years and older	Direct legislative plebiscite

Figure 7.1: Things Change

Local Rules

*"It almost seems that those who have yet to discover the known
are particularly equipped for dealing with the unknown."*

—ERIC HOFFER

Many rules are local. The sun rising every morning is a local phenomenon. At the poles, the sun doesn't always rise, or set. An astronaut in orbit sees many sunrises in a "day." If one were to move away from earth's orbit, the sun would always be up.

The local nature of rules is always getting people into trouble. In the 1950s, then Vice President Nixon went on a goodwill tour to Latin America. The United States was very unpopular in the region at the time, so Nixon wanted to make a good impression. Emerging from the airplane, he grinned, and holding his hands high over his head, touched his forefinger to his thumb, a gesture communicating "OK" in the United States. His audience understood the local meaning—"screw you"—and reacted violently. Remember, what is true in one place is not necessarily true every place.

Traditions Masquerading as Truth

"This is one of those cases in which the imagination is baffled by the facts."

—WINSTON CHURCHILL

Many traditions have been around for so long, we treat them as facts. But these "truths" vary widely from culture to culture. What is ridiculous in one part of the world may be considered a fundamental truth in another. For example, if two mutually exclusive ideas were presented to you, could both to be true? Of course not, you might say, if you are from one part of the world. But many of the world's cultures accept the contradiction without a qualm. There is no reason to believe that our cultural biases represent absolute truth.

Herd Thinking

"Convictions are more dangerous enemies of truth than lies."

—FRIEDRICH NIETZSCHE

Strong opinions can be very persuasive, even when there is evidence to the contrary. In one study, actors tried to convince test subjects to change their minds about some facts. The subjects were very confident of these facts prior to talking with the actors. But after being subjected to the actors' passionate indoctrination, the participants would pick an answer they knew to be wrong 37 percent of the time.

It is easy to believe an erroneous idea if everyone else believes it too. Despite generations of historical experience to the contrary, we will not believe that the whole world can be wrong, even though it repeatedly is.

Scale

"I have no special gift. I am only passionately curious."

—ALBERT EINSTEIN

Rules often change with the scale of things. Generalizations that work so well at one level, like "objects that are much bigger than you are too heavy to carry," simply aren't true when reduced to the scale of an ant. The physics of Newton worked well for big, slow objects. However, when the scale of an object's size or speed changed dramatically, Newtonian physics broke down. Einstein's rules of physics work over a wider range of circumstances, but they also break down in extreme circumstances. We still have more rules to break.

Human dynamics have similar size-dependent quirks. What works in a small group does not always work in a massive organization. Solutions and problems do not scale nicely. But that does not stop us from trying, and large organizations will often continue implementing old solutions that worked for smaller groups until the situation becomes preposterous.

Self-Modifying Rules

"Nothing is easier than self-deceit. For what each man wishes, that he also believes to be true."

—DEMOSTHENES

Many rules are self-modifying. Their very success causes them to change. A good example of this is oil prices. In the 1970s, analysts forecasted that petroleum prices would continue to go up and up. This forecast seemed based on indisputable facts. Demand would continue to rise; it always had. No new oil was being created, so scarcity would drive petroleum prices higher and higher. If geology and market forces didn't drive oil to astronomical heights, then OPEC would. Climbing oil prices was the rule.

This fact changed the world. Consumers slowed their energy consumption. They felt they had no choice. Producers sharply increased their development of oil reserves. No expense was spared. With demand moderating and supplies flooding the market, prices dropped. OPEC members were as addicted to oil revenues as their customers were dependent on oil. They would not reduce their production and were powerless to influence the price of oil. Prices fell. Many oil wells were shut down. Then prices rose again. It is impossible to say where in the cycle you are now as you read this.

IDENTIFYING YOUR RULES

"Reality is merely an illusion, albeit a very persistent one."

—ALBERT EINSTEIN

Solving the most difficult problems requires that you change the thinking that is preventing a solution—your rules. Even good rules can keep you from solving a problem. Try to draw Figure 7.2 on a sheet of paper without breaking contact between your pen or pencil and the paper. Can you do it? When first asked to do this, most people claim that it is impossible. But it is their own rules that make this problem a challenge.

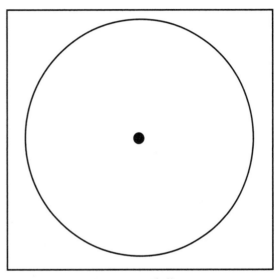

Figure 7.2: A Challenge

We use one side of a sheet of paper at a time. But to draw this figure without lifting your pen, you need to use both sides. Simply draw the center dot and fold a corner of the paper to the dot. Then, without lifting pen from paper, draw along the folded corner, turn ninety degrees and begin drawing your circle. As you draw, your pen will return to the front of the paper, and you will complete the figure without ever breaking contact between pen and paper. If you hadn't been drawing on paper all your life, this would be a simple problem. Your years of excellent experience made it difficult.

The first step in rule breaking is identifying your rules. We will start with the limitations that you identified when you defined your problem. Perceived limitations are often the prime rules that keep us from solutions. Examine your list of limitations. If you listed money as a limitation, than you must have a rule that specifies that a certain amount of money is needed to solve the problem. Extract rules for each of the limitations

117

you listed. Create a list of your rules for solving the problem. List all of your rules, especially the ones that you think can't be broken. Rules that "can't" be broken are at the core of most impossible problems.

You still have more rules about your problem. While you were breaking your patterns of thinking, you created a number of ideas. Some were good and some were awful. Your judgment of those ideas is based on rules. Make rules out of the reasons for embracing or rejecting those ideas. Examine the ideas on your idea sheet. Start with your best ones. What are the reasons behind your judgment? These reasons are more of your rules. List these rules on your rule sheet. You should also have some ideas that you believe will not work. Identify the reasons why they will fail. They are rules too. Record them. For example, you may have rejected an idea as too risky. Implicitly, you have a rule that only low-risk projects are acceptable solutions. Or if the solutions you think are viable require a large team, one of your rules may be that the problem is too big for one person.

Procedures and rules of thumb are excellent candidates for rule breaking. There once may have been a good reason for requiring thirteen vice presidents to sign off on a change, but the reason could have disappeared. Include every procedure that is hindering you in your list.

Don't worry if your rules seem obvious. Many of them will be so obvious that you will be tempted not to include them in your list. Obvious rules are good rules to break. No one has seriously considered violating these rules, while the obvious solutions have failed repeatedly.

Create a long list of rules. Then select one to break. Is there a rule that, if broken, would enable you to solve your problem? This is a keystone rule. Never mind that it can't be broken. It may be just the rule that is standing in your way.

A keystone rule might be that "Greedy, selfish people won't help end hunger." If you could break that rule, you could end hunger. Greedy, selfish people have more than enough resources to do so. If there is no rule that you could break to solve your problem, identify more fundamental rules. Do a pattern-breaking exercise to broaden your thinking. Look for

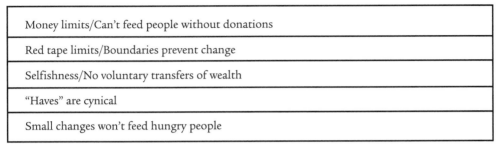

| Money limits/Can't feed people without donations |
| Red tape limits/Boundaries prevent change |
| Selfishness/No voluntary transfers of wealth |
| "Haves" are cynical |
| Small changes won't feed hungry people |

Figure 7.3: Rules

that keystone rule. It will be there if you have an enabling problem. When you have identified your keystone rule, it is time for the most important step in thinking like Einstein: break that rule.

RULE-BREAKING TECHNIQUES

"Men occasionally stumble over the truth, but most of them pick themselves up and hurry off as if nothing happened."

—WINSTON CHURCHILL

Breaking rules is never easy. Violating the rules that are keeping you from your solution requires creativity and intelligence. You must also ignore common sense and have some fun. I like to apply one of four techniques to rules I need to break. They are very simple, and they will work for any rule. I will show how they have been used to get around some important rules, like the law of gravity. I am not suggesting that you jump from a tall building. These are serious rules, humorlessly enforced. But many talented people have worked hard to break these rules and succeeded.

Violate the Rule

Flagrant violations of rules are simple—you break the rule and dare the consequences. It is the essential strategy when nothing else works. A flagrant violation demands boldness. It requires an "I don't care about the facts, nothing will stand in my way" attitude.

During his civil war with Pompeii for the dictatorship of Rome, Julius Caesar was faced with a dilemma where a flagrant violation was the only option. Caesar's rival Pompeii was in Rome, gathering power and support. Caesar and his armies were in distant Gaul, far removed from the levers of power. The solution was obvious—drive Pompeii from Rome. But Caesar could only do that with an army, and entering Italy with an army was an act of rebellion that would enable Pompeii to mobilize all the might of Rome against Caesar. Caesar would be forced to fight a superior force in strong defensive positions, a serious violation of the pragmatic rules of warfare.

It seems like another unsolvable problem. But Caesar adroitly realized that his only choice was to take Rome. Violating the rules that you should not attack a stronger defensive force or make your opponent stronger, Caesar crossed the Rubicon into Italy proper with a single legion. Plunging towards death or destiny, he came up with a strategy. Moving quickly, he eliminated resistance before it could solidify and used early successes to add supporters. Soon Caesar controlled Rome, the only way to win. He would have only been a footnote in history had he not had the courage to break the rules.

Gravity is ignored all the time. We jump from fences, jump into pools. We know there is risk, but we take our chances. People have even survived falls from airplanes and tall buildings. It doesn't happen often, but it is proof that flagrant violations can work even in extreme cases.

No rule is inviolable. It would seem to be a firm rule that a plant species that does not produce seeds or shoots will die out. But there is a family of orange trees that have been successful in breaking this rule. Years ago, a branch of a single orange tree was found that produced seedless oranges. Orange growers have made it their business to help this sterile mutation to propagate. Rather than being doomed to extinction, seedless oranges have become a common variety. All rules can be broken.

How would you flagrantly break your rule? Don't worry about being clever or cunning. Just break the rule.

> **Rule:** Small changes won't feed hungry people.

How can you turn breaking your rule into a solution? Record the idea. It will not be a complete solution. It may not even seem like a good idea. But it is a start.

> **Violate the Rule:** Promote prosperity by making small changes.

Circumvent the Rule

The second technique is to circumvent the rule by avoiding its penalty. Circumventing rules is a kind of stealth rule breaking. You go around the rule by changing the consequence. You still break the rule, but don't get hurt.

Adrenaline addicts skirt the painful consequences of the law of gravity by jumping out of airplanes with parachutes strapped to their backs. They still fall to earth, but descend the last few thousand feet slowly enough to avoid injury.

President Franklin Roosevelt tried to circumvent the rules when the Supreme Court struck down many of his New Deal programs. He couldn't oppose the court directly. The Supreme Court is one of the most immovable of American institutions. So he tried to pack the court, increasing the number of justices until enough of his people were on the court to give him a majority. It didn't work, but it was a creative solution to an impossible problem.

Find a way to circumvent your rule. Be clever about it. Slip around the obstacles. Be legalistic and exploit a trivial loophole. Ask a devious friend for advice. But do what you must to nullify the rule.

> **Rule:** Money limits/Can't feed people without donations.

Record your idea for circumventing your rule as a solution seed. Remember, there are no bad ideas, only ideas whose solution hasn't come.

> **Circumvent the Rule:** Find a source of money other than aid money.

Adopt an Opposite Rule

A great, counterintuitive way to break a rule is to create a new opposite rule, and follow it. This is not as absurd as it appears. The opposite rule to "You must pay taxes" is "The government must pay you." To comply with this new rule, find a way to get the government to give you money. Many have successfully used this strategy to avoid being net tax contributors. In some countries they number a third of the potential work force.

This strategy is not limited to Byzantine rules and convoluted bureaucracies. Physicist Richard Feynman won his Noble prize when he and others asked, "What would happen if just the opposite were true?" It turned out that their new counterintuitive rule made much better sense of the universe.

Businesses once adhered religiously to the idea that economies of scale were the key to competitive success. Factories, airplanes, and organizations grew bigger and bigger to improve efficiencies. Then some discovered that the opposite rule also worked. Smaller factories, airplanes, and organizations nimbly exploited opportunities that bigger competitors could not touch.

Adopting the opposite rule even works on the law of gravity. Balloonists use gravity's pull to thrust themselves into the sky. Gravity pulls surrounding air down, pushing the less dense balloon up.

Nature has validated the "opposite rule" strategy in many ways. Cowbirds use an opposite rule strategy in raising their young. The normal rule for raising birds is that the parents must provide for the babies. Cowbirds have changed the rule to "abandon the baby to raise it." Cowbirds lay their eggs in the nest of another bird. The cowbird chick pushes its foster siblings out of the nest, and is raised by its unwitting and hardworking foster parents.

I used an opposite rule to get my kids ready for bed. It used to take me an hour every night to get them in bed. I decided to adopt the opposite rule: kids can take as long as they want to get ready for bed. Then, to make my opposite rule a solution, I made them start preparing for bed an hour or more early. They could resume playing as soon as they were ready for bed, but not before. The faster they were ready for bed, the more time they had to play. Now they take less than a minute to complete everything.

Formulate a rule that is exactly opposite to the rule you are breaking. Then follow that rule.

Rule: Selfishness/No voluntary transfers of wealth.

And of course, record your idea as the seed of a real solution.

Opposite Rule: The greediest people will feed the hungry.

Special Cases

A popular way to break rules is to create a special exclusionary case. Those that qualify, and they do by design, get to break the rule. Special cases are regularly used to avoid paying taxes. It has been quite legal to exempt oneself from taxes by claiming non-profit status or by doing business in Puerto Rico.

The special case strategy is not confined to legalistic problems. Astronauts seem exempt from the law of gravity while in orbit. Gravity is still there and still pulling, but the astronaut has arranged his trajectory so that gravity can be ignored.

Einstein worked out his special theory of relativity long before his general theory of relativity. By granting himself simple circumstances in his calculations, he was able to find an initial solution. With those new insights, Einstein then solved the more general problem.

Create special circumstances that allow you to break your rule. Exempt yourself from those messy details that make your problem hard to solve. If your problem is ending traffic congestion around a major urban center, then simplify the problem by ignoring private cars. Eliminate the congestion for mass transit passengers. If you could solve this problem efficiently, the bigger problem may take care of itself.

> **Rule:** Red tape limits/Boundaries prevent change.

Record your special circumstances as seeds of real solutions.

> **Special Case:** Make boundaries invisible in key areas.

RULE-BREAKING PRACTICE

"Hell, there are no rules here—we're trying to accomplish something."

—THOMAS EDISON

Until you are a consummate rule breaker, circumventing deeply held patterns will be hard. It will feel uncomfortable, even stupid and heretical. We feel like we are cheating when we break the rules. You will want to skip rule breaking to focus on the more comfortable problem-solving techniques. Don't! If your chosen problem has defied solution for a long time, it is probably because the solution requires violating a common assumption. You must break your rules. If you can't, you need some practice.

Warming Up

Select a rule from the list in Figure 7.4 and think about ways to break it. Use the last digit of your street or apartment number to find the appropriate rule to break. Most are commonly held beliefs or natural laws that may even be among your limiting assumptions. So find your rule and break it.

Last Digit of Address	Rule
0	Murphy's Law (If something can go wrong, it will.)
1	Penny wise and pound foolish
2	Inertia (A body at rest tends to remain at rest.)
3	You can't take it with you.
4	A penny saved is a penny earned.
5	Do it right the first time.
6	The early bird gets the worm.
7	Time moves forward.
8	Buy low, sell high.
9	You can't teach an old dog new tricks.

Figure 7.4: Rule-Breaking Practice

Imagine your street address ended with a nine. How would you teach an old dog new tricks? IBM did. Their costly mainframes faced stiff competition from inexpensive servers. IBM and their mainframes seemed doomed to go the way of the dinosaur. But IBM could learn a new trick. They added server-based computing to their expertise in providing computer services to corporate customers. Now most of IBM's revenue comes from these services, including managing the server farms that replaced their mainframes. Instead of a dying dinosaur, IBM is again a formidable competitor.

Were you successful in breaking your rule? Did you have fun ignoring that stupid limit and doing what you wanted? If you had trouble, you may need to put yourself in the proper rule-busting mood.

Developing the Right Attitude: The James Bond Solution

You need the right attitude to break rules. Picture in your mind someone who solves impossible problems, like James Bond. Picture this competent person without money or friends, in a strange city or country. Give him your problem. Give him your boss or your kids if you really want to make things tough. Would he succeed? Of course he would. He always does, and he would have fun doing it too. You need his attitude.

How would James Bond, or the competent person you selected, attack your problem? Assume his frame of mind. Consider the actions he would take to solve the problem. Where would he go? Who would he talk to? What lucky breaks would happen? How would he have fun?

It is OK to let your imagination run wild. Just capture your thoughts with a few notes. Stay with the exercise until you have guided your very competent person to a solution. While doing this exercise, the competent person probably broke some of the rules that are keeping you from a solution. Why couldn't you do the same thing?

If your problem is settling some crippling patent litigation with a key competitor, solve the problem like a James Bond. Fly to the Caribbean resort you learned he is staying at. Immaculately dressed, you approach him at dinner and offer to settle. When he laughs derisively, coolly offer to throw in a cross license to a new blocking technology. You just created this technology while on the plane and faxed the disclosure to your attorney moments earlier. Then, after he gives in, steal his girlfriend and win the cost of the trip at the casino. You may not want to do all of that, but you could use the blocking technology as the start of a solution.

GOOD RULES TO BREAK

If you are in a rebellious, rule-breaking mood but still can't find a rule to break that will solve your problem, try one of the following. These rules often block good solutions. Use one of the four rule-breaking techniques to find a way, any way, to break these rules.

It's Impossible

"Impossible only means that you haven't found the solution yet."

—UNKNOWN

No one tries to solve impossible problems—they are impossible. The obstacles are too great to even consider a solution. The "it's impossible so don't even try" rule is always a good rule to break, because even impossible problems have been solved.

The Nazi occupation of Poland was horrific. Twenty percent of the Polish people died in forced labor, of hunger, or from fighting. Resistance was impossible. Even the feeblest opposition brought devastating, overwhelming reprisals.

Drs. Lazowski and Matulewicz decided to resist anyway, and their solution was brilliant. They knew that the Germans were terrified of a typhus outbreak. So they injected dead typhus bacteria into various patients, then sent blood samples to the German authorities. The blood tested positive for typhus. The Germans conducted more tests, and most were also positive. The occupation authorities quarantined the area. The people were not deported for slave labor and German troops stayed away. Drs. Lazowski and Matulewicz spared their neighbors the worst of World War II, because even impossible problems have solutions. Make "it's impossible" the first rule you break. Create an opposite rule that your problem will be solved.

Regulations

"That which is not just is not law."

—WILLIAM LLOYD GARRISON

Regulations usually start with good intentions. But they cannot anticipate all future contingencies, so regulations are frequently obstacles to solutions. Einstein faced some insurmountable regulations. He wanted to renounce his German citizenship, but there was no such thing as a stateless person. It just wasn't allowed. He became stateless anyway. He wanted to attend a prestigious scientific university, although he had dropped out of gymnasium, the equivalent of modern-day high school. Gymnasium graduation was essential for acceptance to the highly competitive program. He found a way to be admitted to the university anyway. Regulations can certainly make your solution more difficult, but they can still be broken. If there is a regulation in the way of your solution, ignore it.

Not Enough _____

"Money often costs too much."

—RALPH WALDO EMERSON

Many problems seem impossible because there are not enough resources. There is almost never enough money to do anything right, except useless projects that, by definition, always have more than enough resources committed to them. There are never enough people; there is never enough time. But important things continue to be accomplished. Cities are built, cures are found, and children receive a great education. It is a tragedy when important ideas are not acted on because there wasn't enough of something.

The lack of adequate resources is a real problem. Not just because of the lack, but also because the mind uses inadequate resources as an excuse to stop thinking about solutions. As soon as you believe that there isn't enough, you stop trying to find a solution. To solve an insoluble problem where the resources are inadequate, attack the rule that you can't succeed without them.

One way to attack your lack of resources is to imagine that you had unlimited resources (create an opposite rule). Decide how you would solve your problem if money (or people or knowledge) were no object. List whom you would call, what you would ask for, and what you would do. Every time an obstacle is identified, write a check or assign a body. Then move on to the next obstacle.

Perhaps your boss has assigned you to develop and run a new advertising campaign, but only has given you enough money for the first ad, and no money for development. If money were no obstacle, you would put someone to work on the project. So you interview several advertising firms, including some hungry new ones that may like to get their foot in the door. If you find one that will work for free, you are off to a great start. If not, return to your boss with the best proposal and ask for the money. Or ask more firms for free development work. And keep asking until the ad campaign is created. Then run the only advertisement you have money for, and ask for more money when it is a success.

Seeking solutions as though resources are not an object builds your mental momentum. Your mind becomes accustomed to identifying and disposing of problems. Your internal obstacles to a solution evaporate as you learn to smash through them when they arise.

Just starting a project is often enough to create the intermediate solutions needed to complete it. I once toured Vienna with a couple on their second year of a three-year world tour. They started with only enough money for a plane ticket from New Zealand to San Francisco. But that first step was enough. They had started. They then paid for cars, fares, tours, fun, and musical instruments by occasionally performing or wielding a shovel. They always found a way. They even had a baby, who greatly increased their revenue from street concerts. They were having a wonderful time on a trip that many wealthy people think they can't afford.

Money-is-no-object thinking also can help generate a more practical solution. After you have sketched out a money-is-no-object solution, determine how much each action would cost. Then ask:

▶ Can I afford the solution?

▶ Who could afford the solution?

▶ What would motivate them to pay the bill?

▶ Would it be worth the price?

▶ What portions of the solution can I afford?

▶ Are there any actions I can substitute that I can afford?

Your problem is easier to solve with a plan. Plans come before resources like ideas precede action. Use this as the basis of a plan to win the resources that you need.

The Shortest Distance Doesn't Work

"If I had eight hours to chop down a tree, I'd spend six sharpening my ax."

—ABRAHAM LINCOLN

Problems are often considered insoluble because the direct, obvious route to a solution is impractical. The assumption is that if the direct route doesn't work, indirect routes won't work either. They must be worse.

Is the shortest distance between two points a straight line? Well, consider Federal Express. They found that fastest way to move parcels between two points was to fly them all to the same place for sorting, and then fly them to their final destination. A package destined for a nearby city traveled thousands of miles, but the detour allowed numerous other procedures to be streamlined. The solution focused on the distribution facility rather than the long distances between facilities.

Make a list of all the indirect ways you could approach your problem. To help yourself warm up to the problem, make your first detour as circuitous and bizarre as possible.

It's Been Tried Before

"Nothing quite new is perfect."

—CICERO

Most good ideas must be tried several times before someone finally finds a way to make them work. Mistakes and false starts are almost a precondition of a success. But we forget this. Instead we embrace the notion that something that has failed once cannot be made to work.

If the "it's been tried before" rule were scrupulously followed, we would be without airplanes, democracy, and convertibles. Retrying a failed idea is a good example of the "Violate the Rule" or the "Circumvent the Rule" rule-breaking strategies. A second try may succeed because circumstances have changed or because you avoid repeating the part of the previous effort that caused its failure.

George Kinney's friends probably thought he was crazy when he scraped together every dollar he could find to purchase the inventory of his former, failed employer. If Kinney's old boss had gone bankrupt with those shoes, then surely Kinney would too. But Kinney learned from his boss's mistakes and grew the business, which he renamed Kinney's Shoes, into a fortune.

So what if an idea has failed before? Things are different now. There are new players. You can learn from earlier mistakes. There is a better chance you can make it work this time.

BREAKING YOUR RULES

"Art is either plagiarism or revolution."

—PAUL GAUGUN

You've got to break the rules to solve tough problems. Be bold. Be creative. Be unconventional. Create solutions that assume you can break rules. Breaking rules requires attitude and creativity. If you have the attitude that you can and must break a limiting rule, then unleash your creativity on it. Break your rules, and record all the seeds of possible solutions that come from your violations. The next step in Einstein Thinking is to grow those seeds into real solutions.

CHAPTER EIGHT

Growing a Solution

> "It's not that
> I'm smart, it's just
> that I stay with the
> problems longer."
>
> —ALBERT EINSTEIN

Einstein's theory of relativity was almost proven wrong. In 1914, relativity's predictions were still wrong, even after years of work. That year, German scientists planned to verify the theory by observing light being bent during an eclipse in Russia. The observation would have shown Einstein to be wrong because his theory would have incorrectly predicted the bending of light. His idea was still brilliant, but the details were incomplete. Relativity would have been discredited if World War I hadn't postponed the planned test. Einstein spent four more years growing his idea into a real solution. His much-improved theory was validated during a 1918 eclipse.

Even brilliant ideas require much creative work to become solutions. Now that you have broken out of your rut, defied your rules, and created the seeds of some solutions, you must grow one of those seeds into a real solution. There is still much innovation to be done, and the first step is to focus on one idea.

SELECTING ONE SOLUTION

"The only reason for time is so that everything doesn't happen at once."

—ALBERT EINSTEIN

You may be reluctant to focus on any single idea when you have many interesting options. But growing a solution requires laser-like intensity. You cannot "focus" simultaneously on multiple different ideas. You must choose one.

Selecting an idea is a form of judgment. Your judgment is biased by your rules. Using good judgment will quickly eliminate all the novel ideas. Instead, eliminate the solutions that conform to your rule rut. When you were defining the problem, you identified your three best current options, the best not-good-enough solutions. They are still off-limits. So are similar ideas. Unless you have a compelling twist, you will fall back into your rule rut by using them.

Choose to develop the idea that is most exciting to you. Your interest is the selection criteria. Don't eliminate an idea because it is unworkable or weak. That may just be your prejudices again, veering you away from a

Solution Seeds	
	Get people from wealthy nations to move to poor nations for mutual advantage.
X	Remove barriers to people in impoverished areas to improve their own circumstances.
	Promote prosperity by making small changes.
	Find a source of money other than aid money.
	Have greedy people feed the hungry.
	Make boundaries invisible in key areas.
Target Solution	
	Eliminate barriers to prosperity.

Figure 8.1: Selecting a Solution

revolutionary thought. Reject boring ideas because you won't work hard enough to make them successful. The seed idea that excites you is your target solution. Write it down.

Focus your problem solving energies on making this solution work.

GREAT IDEAS NEED TO GROW

"Genius is the ability to hold one's vision steady until it becomes a reality."

—BENJAMIN FRANKLIN

Congratulations! You have a potential solution. Unfortunately, you still face a few small problems—your solution doesn't work and everyone thinks it is stupid.

Don't worry! You are in good company. Breakthroughs seldom work the first time and great ideas are rejected by almost everyone. It took the Wright Brothers years after their first successful flight to interest anyone in their airplane, and their idea changed the world in their lifetime.

Your new thinking will be rejected for one of two reasons. First, you may be completely wrong. That is not as bad as it sounds. Useless ideas, or Chris Concepts, are fertile ground for new solutions. At worst you have created associations, connections, and ideas in your mind that can be used again on something that will work. Failure provides a clearer idea of where to explore next and a thorough understanding of something that doesn't work. The only real tragedy of a failure occurs if it stops you from trying again.

The second possibility is that your idea may only look completely wrong. A real breakthrough will seem useless because it has much growing and refining ahead of it. Great ideas do not spring forth fully developed. Instead they appear as conceptual infants, full of promise but far from ready to stand on their own.

Richard Feynman gave a classic example of why good ideas always seem so stupid. Meso-Americans were great astronomers. They had primitive ideas about the structure of the solar system, but generations of sightings and corrections allowed them to make accurate predictions of eclipses and other phenomena. Imagine going to the chief astronomer and saying, "I've got a great idea. We are on a planet that is one of many planets revolving around the sun. Let's reconstruct astronomy around this beautiful concept!"

The chief astronomer would then ask, "Can your theory predict eclipses?"

You reply, "Well, no, not yet. But I am sure it will give us more accurate predictions after I have developed it over many years." Imagine the response that would get!

You can be confident that your breakthrough ideas are either wrong or just appear wrong. Unfortunately, you cannot distinguish which without more work. You must grow your idea until it is robust enough to determine if it is a good one.

PATIENCE: SUSPENDING JUDGMENT

"Whoever undertakes to set himself up as a judge in the field of knowledge and truth is shipwrecked by the laughter of the Gods."

—ALBERT EINSTEIN

"Sticking to it is the genius."

—THOMAS EDISON

Growing an idea requires patience. Einstein's theory of relativity was almost proven wrong before it could be made right, but many great ideas are not so lucky. After an early failure, they languish until someone picks them up and moves them a little farther forward.

There is record of an eleventh century monk named Eilmer who built and tested a primitive glider. He is said to have glided for hundreds of meters. If true, it was a stunning breakthrough. But his contemporaries viewed the flight as a complete failure because Eilmer had trouble controlling his glider. He crashed and was seriously injured. Therefore, in their minds, it must have been a stupid idea.

Facts and experts are deadly to new thinking. They highlight the flaws, gaps, and obstacles that abound in all great ideas. They can make anything seem ridiculous. You must suspend your own judgment and protect your idea from others until you can develop it into a robust solution.

Developing a brilliant idea takes much patient effort. Numerous obstacles will plague even the most promising ideas before they can become real solutions. Mahon Loomis demonstrated a wireless telegraph in 1868. Guglielmo Marconi's first wireless transmission wasn't until 1895. But Loomis was unable to overcome the financial obstacles to promulgating his invention. He finally gave up. Marconi had the same problems. But he stuck with it, and changed the world.

Ignore Inconvenient Facts

"How much easier it is to be critical than to be correct."

—BENJAMIN DISRAELI

You will find many reasons why your idea won't work. You will be tempted to abandon your own breakthrough. Don't let the facts get in the way of your solution. Adopt the attitude that you must make your concept work, regardless of obstacles. Every other assumption, rule, and convention can be ignored, except for your idea. If you find an obstacle to your idea, then the obstacle must go. Favor your new idea over all other facts.

Miranda Stuart did not let the facts get in the way when she decided to become a physician. Miranda was barred from studying medicine because she was a woman. But she wanted to practice medicine desperately, and wasn't about to let reality stand in her way. So she graduated from the Edinburgh College of medicine as a man. She then entered military service, and even served as surgeon general of Canada. The fact that Dr. Stuart could not be a doctor was irrelevant.

You must stick with your idea fanatically to find out if it is a good one. When you encounter a "fact" that makes your solution impossible, record it. Use rule-breaking techniques to make your solution work anyway.

Inconvenient Facts	Violate the Rule	Circumvent the Rule	Opposite Rule	Special Case
The industry standard uses a completely different approach.			X	
Current federal laws prohibit this merger.				X
My teenager won't enforce his own curfew.		X		
Someone at my level can't talk with the CEO about new ideas.	X			

Figure 8.2: Inconvenient Facts

When asked what he would have done if experiments had not confirmed his theory of relativity, Einstein responded, "I would have been obliged to pity our dear God. The theory is correct." This response exemplifies the attitude you must have to grown an idea into a solution. You will never know whether you had a great breakthrough or a Chris Concept until you have persevered with your idea.

Challenging the Experts

"I know that most men, including those at ease with problems of the greatest complexity, can seldom accept even the simplest and most obvious truth if it be such as would oblige them to admit the falsity of conclusions which they have delighted in explaining to colleagues, which they have proudly taught to others, and which they have woven, thread by thread, into the fabric of their lives."

—LEO TOLSTOY

Experts are tough on new ideas. They prefer their facts. Ideas that challenge their facts are threats. If the new concept catches on, then they are no longer experts. Experts have killed many great ideas.

Alfred Wegner was a smart man. He was trained as an astronomer and a meteorologist, and had practical experience as a polar explorer. However, he had no credentials as a geophysicist. This was unfortunate because he made a remarkable contribution to geophysics.

Alfred Wegner had a great idea, a true breakthrough. He noticed that the continental shelves of North and South America and those of Europe and Africa fit together like the pieces of a puzzle. Even the geologic formations along the respective coasts matched. Wegner was certain that the continents had once been one large continent before drifting apart. It was brilliant thinking.

But as Wegner explained his infant idea to the experts, he made some mistakes. Expert geophysicists eagerly jumped on these minor errors. They tore apart the undeveloped concepts, completely discrediting the most significant advance in their field. As a result, Wegner's breakthrough died with him.

Decades later, geophysical science had progressed enough that Wegner's idea of moving continents was again proposed, this time by geophysicists. By then the weight of evidence was indisputable. Wegner's idea is now the basis of geophysics. Modern textbooks explain the theory, but often fail to mention that a meteorologist first proposed the idea.

Even the smartest people can be very wrong. Isaac Newton forcefully opposed attempts to use clocks to determine longitude. He thought accurate sea-going clocks were impractical. Fortunately, John Harrison was not afraid to disagree with the greatest mind of the age. It took him several iterations over many years, but he ultimately perfected a small, accurate clock that was not affected by the rolling of ships, temperature change, or winding. It was the technology of choice for calculating longitude for hundreds of years until satellite-based positioning began to replace it.

Experts are proficient in conventional knowledge, but they have a poor record of recognizing great new ideas:

"Louis Pasteur's theory of germs is ridiculous fiction." —Pierre Pachet, professor of physiology, 1872

"This 'telephone' has too many shortcomings to be seriously considered as a means of communication. The device is inherently of no value to us." —Internal Western Union memo, 1876

"Heavier-than-air flying machines are impossible." —Lord Kelvin, president of the Royal Society, 1895

"Who the hell wants to hear actors talk?" —H.M. Warner of Warner Brothers, 1927

"We don't like their sound, and guitar music is on the way out." —Decca Recording Company on the Beatles, 1962

Don't despair when every expert ridicules your ideas. Once, one hundred Nazi professors wrote a book attacking Einstein's theories. Einstein just shrugged it off saying, "If I were wrong, one professor would have been enough." Experts will have plenty of reasons to discount your concept. They will convince themselves (and try to convince you) that you are crazy. You must be committed if you are going to grow your idea into a solution.

To deflect the derision of experts from your idea, don't tell them. If the experts find out, call it a learning exercise. You don't expect it to succeed, but you do expect to learn something interesting from the failure. Shame them with their lack of curiosity. Then make it work. The experts will eventually come around. Dr. Barbara McClintock finally won the Nobel prize for medicine after her revolutionary work on genes jumping within a chromosome had been ignored for thirty years. It took that long for the "experts" to understand what she had done.

SEX

"The secret to creativity is knowing how to hide your sources."

—ALBERT EINSTEIN

Sex is good for ideas. The overwhelming majority of ideas that have been developed on earth are in the gene pool, embodied in actual living things—their cells, eyes, and muscles. And the best genes come from sex. Even simple one-celled animals try to swap DNA when possible.

Why is sex so great? Not because it is easy to do. Species that reproduce sexually incur huge risks, expend enormous amounts of energy, or, in the case of humans, money, for the chance to intermingle some genetic material. The need to perpetuate one's DNA does not fully explain the need for sex. Asexual reproduction is simpler and passes on all of an organism's genes instead of just half. It would seem the natural strategy for self-perpetuating DNA. Instead these selfish genes have selected sex.

A billion years of developing great DNA has shown that sex is worth the trouble. Organisms that reproduce sexually, sharing the precious DNA in their offspring with a mate, are much more advanced than species that reproduce asexually. And animals that can reproduce asexually, like bacteria and turkeys, favor some form of sexual reproduction when possible. Sex combines two successful sets of genetic material to create something new. Sometimes it is much better. These differences have been so successful that the natural world is solidly committed to sex.

Sex works for ideas too. The cerebral version of sex, or cerebral sex, is as important to creating successful solutions as biological sex is to successful organisms. Cerebral sex is a one- or two-way exchange of ideas. It includes collaboration, borrowing an idea or learning from another's mistake. It can be intentional or subconscious. And it is much more efficient and effective than developing your idea alone.

Great ideas are rarely the work of one person, though one person often gets the credit. Darwin's grandfather proposed an early theory of evolution. Bell saw an early telephone similar to the one he invented, and the Wright brothers took advantage of years of aerodynamic research. Creative solutions have many parents.

You need outside thinking to grow your idea into a robust solution. Fresh ideas strengthen promising solutions. They fill in the gaps and correct the weaknesses. Everything from democracy to grocery stores is regularly inculcated with new concepts that make them better solutions. Cerebral sex makes ideas great.

Einstein benefited from sharing ideas. He grew and developed his great ideas with the help of many collaborators. He could never have done as much working alone.

One advantage that geniuses often acquire is access to better cerebral sex. They have the opportunity to talk with many other bright people. With frequent exchanges of ideas, their thinking potential is expanded even more. To develop better ideas faster, you must do the same, and engage in more cerebral sex.

Nature teaches us another important lesson about growing great ideas—avoid incest. Nature favors behaviors that avoid incest because inbreeding makes poor genes. You must reduce intellectual incest as you exchange ideas to grow your solution. Collaborating with someone in your field or with your education background is good, but highly incestuous. Seek advice from those with different professions, backgrounds, and biases.

Growing your idea into a solution will require lots of cerebral sex. Share ideas with at least ten different people and record the ideas that are conceived. And keep the incest level low. You may want to keep track of your idea exchanges to help you recognize if your thinking is getting enough cerebral sex. For example, if you were working on some new airline routes into Europe, you might keep a log like the one in Figure 8.3.

Unfortunately, nature has not given us a sex-like drive to share ideas. Instead we hoard ideas. We are reluctant to discuss our thinking because we fear theft or ridicule. You must overcome your inhibitions to sharing ideas if you are to grow a great solution. Cerebral sex must become as compelling as biological sex.

Collaborator	Incest Level	Ideas
Bob Peters, Detroit	low	Midwest to Stuttgart route
Adel Wood	high	Gate availability
Hanspeter Schiess	low	Seasonal opportunities

Figure 8.3: Idea Log

If you think a partner would benefit your solution, look for a good match. Analyze the skills and personality traits that you have and record them. Determine what skills and traits you will need to be successful. Then find a partner that makes up for what you lack. Your partner should be strong where you are weak.

You and your partner should be tolerant of each other. This is more important than finding a smart partner. Einstein left his brilliant first wife for one who was much more tolerant of his inattention. Partnerships are never easy. You may not ever find a good partner. But it is worth looking. When partnerships click, they are extremely productive.

MISTAKES—THE MILESTONES TO SOLUTIONS

"Anyone who has never made a mistake has never tried anything new."

—ALBERT EINSTEIN

Mistakes are essential to growing ideas. You don't want to make mistakes deliberately, but you can't find a breakthrough solution without them. Mistakes are evidence that you are pushing the boundaries of your solution. We do things perfectly when we have done them before. We make mistakes when we are trying something new. Einstein Thinking requires experiments to succeed, and so it requires mistakes. If everything you try succeeds, you are extremely conservative in your thinking.

It took many mistakes for Paul Caffe, a poor African American living in colonial America, to become the proud owner of a fleet of merchant ships. Pirates captured Caffe's first boat. He lost the second when he couldn't sell the cargo. But Caffe learned from every mistake. His third boat was the first of numerous successes. Many ships and mistakes later, Paul Caffe had his own fleet.

Try as many experiments as possible to make your solution work. You will generate lots of Chris Concepts. From one of those failures will come success. Record each trial and what you learned to be sure you make enough mistakes to succeed.

Experiment	Date	What Was Learned
Bob Peters, Detroit	low	Midwest to Stuttgart route
Gave product away to generate publicity.	4/1	Publicity was good, but riot was bad. Move promotion away from store and don't run out!
Gave away certificates at several high-traffic locations.	4/15	Store too busy redeeming certificates after promotion to actually sell. Stagger redemption.
Distributed small numbers of certificates daily over two weeks.	4/29	Traffic and sales up!

Figure 8.4: Experiment Log

Experiments are a good way to sift through all that is useless about an idea and extract the valuable solution. Marie and Pierre Curie's discovery of radium amounted to sifting through tons of rock to refine the tiny quantity of radium they believed must be there. Besides winning the Curies a Nobel prize, radium was crucial to many other advances, including some by Einstein, that depended upon a reliable source of radiation.

Intellectually, we know that it is OK to make mistakes. Avoiding mistakes is avoiding progress. But because mistakes are painful, embarrassing, and expensive, we still try to avoid making them. To grow your infant idea into a strong solution, you must make lots of mistakes. Get over your aversion to error. You will be able to make more mistakes if you learn to minimize the pain, or to ignore the anguish when you do make a mistake.

Thought Experiments

"Experience is the name everyone gives to their mistakes."

—OSCAR WILDE

Einstein loved thought experiments. He was almost seriously hurt pushing the mechanical limits of a student experiment, so he chose to perform later tests in the safety of his mind. Einstein created mental problems to explore ideas. These experiments were often fanciful, like riding a beam of light or manually separating two subatomic particles. Both of these tasks are impossible, but Einstein learned much by thinking through the implications of each.

Thought experiments allow you to test an idea without expense or embarrassment. It is confined to your head. You don't fall, lose the children's college fund, or look like a fool, but you can still learn much about your solution.

Thought experiments are bold. They are most enlightening at the extremes. A good thought experiment applies the solution to the whole world, or to one individual. It assumes infinite resources or no resources. If you were looking for a way to cut assembly costs by 10 percent, your thought experiment should focus on cutting costs by 100 percent. How would you eliminate all assembly costs? You could buy the components assembled, mold the whole assembly as a unit, or eliminate the need for the unit. Your solutions don't need to be completely realistic. But as you work through the extreme problem, you will learn much.

Create a thought experiment to test your idea. Imagine an extreme situation involving the new concepts that you have been working with. Identify the issues you must address to make your solution work in this situation. "Observe" what happens as you perform your experiment. Solve the problems that arise any way you can. Make your mistakes in this painless environment, and use the confidence you gain from working out the extreme cases to make a real trial of your idea.

Ego, Mistakes, and Progress

"The only source of knowledge is experience."

—ALBERT EINSTEIN

It is hard to think of Dr. Albert Einstein, one of history's most brilliant minds, as a smart aleck kid. But he was. He cut class, made fun of his professors, and violated school rules. His impudent stunts set his education and career back years. Einstein made these mistakes because he had a big head. He knew that he was much smarter than anyone else was. He went head to head with the authorities even when he was guaranteed to lose, driving everyone from teachers to Nazis wild with rage. Einstein suffered for it, but he knew he was right.

I am not suggesting it is a good idea to insult the professor whose recommendation is essential to getting the job you want (yes, Einstein did that) or to get yourself expelled from the country (Herr Doctor did that too). But that is the right frame of mind. To grow your solution, and to endure the mistakes that are a natural by-product, you need a bigger ego.

Making mistakes will be embarrassing. It can hurt. It can cost you money. You must feel clever enough, powerful enough, and sure enough of ultimate success that the mistakes you make along the way won't bother you. This may require some practice. Here is an exercise to prepare you for making those vital mistakes.

Heroic Solutions

"Success isn't final and failure isn't fatal."

—WINSTON CHURCHILL

Superheroes can do anything. It may be difficult. They may be wounded while the world teeters on the brink of total disaster, but they will succeed.

To build some Einstein-sized confidence, imagine that you are your favorite comic book hero. You have enormous power. You can do anything. Of course, you pose as a mild-mannered, average guy to your family and friends, but they should be worshipping the ground you walk on. You don't mind. That's the kind of guy or gal you are, the most powerful, brilliant, humble person on the planet.

Visualize how your favorite comic book hero would solve your problem. It is OK to use excessive force—blow away those obstacles. Use your superior intellect, strength, or technology to cut directly through to a solution. Be melodramatic. Revel in the glory of your accomplishment. If you make mistakes, so what? You will triumph in the end.

Would a superhero like you worry about making a few mistakes? Breaking a few windows? Smashing up a city or two? No! The problem

MUST be solved. It is OK to make a few mistakes along the way. It comes with the superhero territory. Carry that attitude into growing your solution.

Daily Risk

"A good plan violently executed today is better than a perfect plan executed tomorrow."

—GEORGE PATTON

One of the thought experiments that Einstein and his colleagues debated involved a cat in a box. Inside the box was a device that would kill the cat when a radioactive particle decayed. The time of the decay could not be fixed in time, so the only way to know if the cat was alive was to look. Besides showing that a few physicists hate cats, the idea was to demonstrate that some outcomes cannot be predicted until they happen.

This is true of ideas. It is hard to know if one will work until you try it, then try it in a different way, then try it again. You must try new things to grow solutions. For the next four weeks, try a new twist to your solution each day. Every day, do a thought experiment or actual trial of some new way to implement your solution. You will make lots of mistakes, but you will also make much progress.

Sunday	Made demo video with clay and blocks.
Monday	Hired valets at six power restaurants to leave my script in the fanciest cars they park.
Tuesday	Posed as dentist's secretary correcting appointments to learn when Max's next dental visit is. Will be waiting.
Wednesday	Rewrote treatment as women's movie.
Thursday	Hired blonde to wear sandwich board with story pitch outside studio.
Friday	Pitched stage version of script to summer theater group.
Saturday	Badgered Max's second grade teacher, old football coach, and three of his children into recommending he read my script.

Figure 8.5: Daily Risk Log

Even when you are not working on a solution, it helps to build a habit of trying new things. Put yourself in a situation where failure is possible. There are all kinds of novel things to try: an aggressive commute route, a different radio station, or a new restaurant are small risks. If you haven't exercised your artistic talent lately, try drawing or sculpting a friend or singing a well-known song very loudly. Doing either in public is a particularly good risk-taking exercise. Every day that you try something new, mark it down on the chart. Let's see how adventurous you can be.

SOLUTIONS FROM IDEAS

"One person with a belief is equal to a force of ninety-nine who have only interest."

—JOHN STUART MILL

Once Einstein and an assistant needed a paper clip. All they could find was a single bent paper clip. Einstein proceeded to try and straighten it, but he needed a tool. He and the assistant searched the office again. This time they found a box of paper clips. Einstein took a paper clip from the box and bent it into a tool to straighten the first paper clip. The assistant asked why Einstein was bothering to repair the paper clip now that they had a whole box. Einstein responded, "Once I am set upon a goal it becomes difficult to deflect me." That is the determination needed to develop great solutions. It will take time and effort to turn a good idea into an answer. You will probably need to break your rules again and again to solve the new problems that will arise while you are solving the first one. Ultimately, you may even need to concede that you have hit a dead end and start again.

Starting over is often an important part of problem solving. It is so critical that we should recognize it for what it really is, reassessing the problem anew in light of what was learned from the last attempt at a solution. Even when starting over you are making progress towards finding a solution.

A failed solution may always be a Chris Concept with successful application outside of your original target problem. John Wesley Hyatt invented a roller bearing that he knew was perfect for the wheels of railroad cars. It probably was, but railroads weren't interested. Oiled rags seemed to be working just fine as railroad wheel bearings. Since the only significant wheeled industry wasn't buying, Hyatt gave up and sold his business, cheap, to a young man named Alfred Sloan. Sloan sold the roller bearings to the infant automotive industry that needed rugged wheel bearings to cope with rutted roads. He made a fortune supplying Henry Ford before he broke a few other rules and ended up dominating the automobile industry as head of General Motors.

CHAPTER NINE

Avoiding Martyrdom

"Great spirits have
always encountered
violent opposition from
mediocre minds."

—ALBERT EINSTEIN

MARTYRPHOBIC RULES

Einstein's talent for breaking rules was not always appreciated. Einstein clashed repeatedly with academic and scientific authorities before becoming an international scientific superstar. And even when he was safe from the attacks of mediocre scientific minds, Einstein was harassed for his forward-looking political ideas. Driven from Nazi Germany into asylum in the United States, he continued to clash with the political establishment over issues of intellectual expression and nuclear war. Einstein saw clearly the madness in the Cold War and any resolution short of peace. He was one of the few people brave enough to condemn Senator McCarthy's inquisition, urging other intellectuals to refuse to appear before investigating committees. It is fortunate that Einstein was left relatively unscathed for all his novel thinking. Many are not so lucky. Martyrdom is an occupational hazard of great thinkers. If you have conceived a great idea, you must also have a strategy to avoid suffering for it.

The fear of being martyred for your idea is a subtle but real obstacle to Einstein Thinking. You may avoid breaking key rules, growing a solution, or even honestly defining the problem because you fear the consequences. This is not an irrational fear.

Thinking something new can be perilous. Copernicus was brilliant enough to figure out that the earth revolved around the sun. He was also clever enough to avoid punishment for his great contribution. He distributed his work anonymously. Scholars around Europe benefited from his thinking, and Copernicus was allowed to live. The martyrdom scenario is repeated with sickening regularity throughout history. An important idea is branded as heresy, treason, or quackery. The discoverer suffers various injustices: death, prison, dismissal, or transfer to oblivion. Then the idea is adopted. And sometimes the creator is honored posthumously, although credit often goes to those who tried to kill the idea.

Einstein Thinking seeks solutions by violating established assumptions. When using it, your intelligence, at the very least, will be questioned. If you are not careful, you will be derided, demoted, ostracized, transferred, fired, jailed, or shot, depending on whose rules you are breaking.

But why risk harm for your contribution? Great solutions should be beneficial, especially to you. An important and often neglected aspect of great thinking is avoiding martyrdom. Your idea will be more successful if you can mitigate the personal negative consequences. You will also be more creative if you know it won't hurt. This chapter will explain techniques for avoiding martyrdom when using Einstein Thinking.

Understanding the Resistance

"Two things are infinite: the universe and human stupidity,
and I'm not sure about the universe."

—Albert Einstein

Good ideas will be resisted. Rational, intelligent people will fight against brilliant, insightful, and correct thinking. We have already discussed that great ideas start as skinny, weak, underdeveloped ideas. But even after your thinking has grown into a solid concept, you may encounter opposition because even the worst situations benefit someone. They have a vested interest in maintaining things as they are. They will fight to preserve it, probably from a position of power. Even when radically new thinking would seem to benefit the existing power base, it can seem threatening. The powerful are masters of the old thinking. They might be less knowledgeable, less connected, less necessary in the world if the new idea was put in place.

New ideas can also be bad ideas. Some changes should be opposed. But progress is an uphill battle. The slow decline of the command economy, or communism, provides several good examples of the resistance to a better idea by an entrenched power base.

Persistent Bad Ideas

"In order to be an immaculate member of a flock of sheep,
one must above all be a sheep oneself."

—ALBERT EINSTEIN

Communism was an obvious economic failure, particularly in the side-by-side comparison states of Germany, Korea, and China. So why did command economies persist? The simple answer is that those who benefited from communism also had the guns. They prevented beneficial change to maintain their own advantage.

But it isn't just communists that have had trouble changing. Resistance to change is universal. The Western reaction to the decline of communism is a classic example of self-interest triumphing over reality. The evidence mounted for years that communist economies were collapsing at accelerating rates. A junior analyst with the most basic grasp of history should have seen that dramatic political changes were a real possibility. Many probably did. But intelligence organizations ignored these possibilities. Data was "adjusted" so that the communists looked as frightening as ever. They needed the Red Menace to justify their existence.

When the Red Menace was publicly coming apart and Eastern Europe hung in the balance, Western governments still could not change. They continued to spend a billion dollars each to more efficiently fight a war that would destroy the whole planet. Only token sums could be found to help millions of old enemies become friends. There were no well-connected beneficiaries of aid to struggling democracies, but plenty of important defense contractors.

DEAD RIGHT

"It is really a puzzle what drives one to take one's work so devilishly seriously."

—ALBERT EINSTEIN

If better ideas were so obvious, why didn't people in Western defense agencies say, "This is stupid! Let's do things radically differently"? Maybe they did. We may never know how much dissent existed. Organizations silence dissenters. Whether it is jail, transfer, termination, or isolation, the purveyors of unpopular ideas tend to disappear. You can imagine what happens to the guy who says, "My analysis indicates that we are not really needed." Being right is no protection from bureaucratic revenge.

Billy Mitchell was an early American proponent of air power. After World War I, he made all sorts of wild claims about aircraft controlling the seas and devastating cities. He even demonstrated some of his claims, sinking a surplus warship. Mitchell was right, but being right didn't advance his career. He was called before a court martial for tirelessly advocating the future. Mitchell's opponents were never tried for stupidity.

AVOIDING THE HERETIC'S FATE

"If A is success in life, then A = x + y + z.
Work is x, y is play, z is keeping your mouth shut."

—ALBERT EINSTEIN

People clever enough to create solutions also understand the political risks inherent in rocking the boat. You know what happens to the bearers of bad news. So many innovators censor themselves. They hide their ideas to protect themselves. This must not be. We need those solutions. Your fear of punishment for your idea could be a major obstacle to growing it into a great solution. Here are four strategies for escaping martyrdom due to thinking like Einstein.

Give Someone Else the Idea, and the Credit

Benjamin Franklin suggested this wise and selfless strategy. Instead of enthusiastically supporting your own idea, pretend it came from someone else. Then enthusiastically support it. Assigning credit is especially effective if the idea is attributed to a powerful person.

This strategy works well for two reasons. First, it removes the suspicion and jealousy that you are supporting the idea because it is your own. Second, people support their own ideas. If you make your idea their idea, they will fight for it.

Giving others the credit will line up all those egos so that they support you. Ego reigns supreme over reason. Some people will do almost anything to avoid a perceived inferior position. Egos inflate auction prices and add billions to the cost of corporate deals. And when the ego of a national leader becomes involved, the cost can be incalculable. Millions have died so the big guy doesn't look bad.

It isn't hard to transfer your breakthrough to someone else. Just engage your boss in a conversation. Work through your thinking on making the product appealing for younger customer segments. Suggest your idea of a new youth brand as though you hadn't seriously considered it. When she comments on it, get visibly excited. Tell her that she has added the key piece to the puzzle. Then spread "her" idea around the company. Become an enthusiastic supporter.

Use Fear

Another strategy for deflecting the retribution for a good idea is to give a competitor the credit for your innovation. If your problem was finding ways to differentiate your bank, then attribute your solutions to gossip about your competitors. Say you heard that the rival bank is considering twenty-four-hour teller service. Then express doubts about the idea, but point out how damaging it would be if the idea worked with busy high-income people and your organization were not prepared. People are much more fearful of losing to the competition than they are of losing an opportunity. Your colleagues will consider anything they believe a competitor might try. Create competitive threat to spur consideration of your idea.

Create a Benefit for the Powerful

"He that dies a martyr proves that he was not a knave,
but by no means that he was not a fool."

—CHARLES COLTON, SPORTSMAN AND WRITER

Your idea will be more rapidly accepted if the powers that be recognize the benefits to them. There are people who will selflessly champion a breakthrough even to their own detriment. But don't count on finding one at your inquisition.

Behind every big change is a big severance package. In Eastern Europe, diehard apparatchiks finally abandoned communism to become rich. They sold state assets to themselves, maintaining their privileged positions while changing systems. Communism would have never crumbled if the apparatchiks were turned out into the street.

Create a benefit to the powerful as a key part of your breakthrough. Today's authorities must be better off.

Allow an Outsider to Break the News

The explosion of the Space Shuttle Challenger seemed an unsolvable mystery. A blue-ribbon panel of experts was convened to determine what had gone wrong and why. Einstein probably would have been asked if he were alive, but another genius, Richard Feynman, was included. Feynman reviewed the wreckage and scrutinized the films. He read stacks of reports and listened to armies of witnesses. But the cause of the explosion still eluded him.

Of course, the actual cause of the explosion was known inside NASA almost immediately. The only real problem in unraveling the Challenger mystery was how to break the news. No one was willing to compound the tragedy of the disaster with the tragedy of destroying his career. Finally, an Air Force general who had been secretly told what went wrong invited Feynman to his home to look at a weekend project. The general planted the hint, cold O-ring seals, and Feynman's fertile mind solved the mystery. Feynman quickly demonstrated his breakthrough: the shuttle's cold O-ring seals had shattered. Challenger's unusually cold O-rings must have allowed hot gases from the solid rocket boosters to escape, triggering the explosion. The mystery was solved.

The need for outsiders to break bad news drives much of the consulting industry. Unlike insiders, consultants look best when they can point out serious problems. Surveys, polls, and focus groups are also safe ways to break bad news. The voice of the people is the voice of God, and who wants to argue with God?

Anonymous disclosure is a less attractive way of breaking bad news. It does get the idea out, but reflects poorly on the idea itself. And you can't easily support an anonymous idea. Attribute your idea to someone else rather than releasing it anonymously.

But by all means, circulate your breakthrough concept. Give others the chance to refine it, poke holes in it. Your idea needs cerebral sex to develop. Just don't get yourself hanged in the process.

Your Strategy

"Although prepared for martyrdom, I preferred that it be postponed."
—WINSTON CHURCHILL

"The first duty of a revolutionary is to get away with it."
—ABBIE HOFFMAN

To grow your idea into a solution, you need a way to avoid the negative consequences of innovation. Create a strategy that will allow you to actively develop the idea, gather support, and avoid inquisitions. After you have your strategy, stick with it. The solution is more important than the glory.

> **Strategy for Avoiding Martyrdom:** Sign up a VIP as figurehead for the project.

CLAIMING YOUR DUE

"Morality is all right, but what about dividends?"

—KAISER WILHEM

These ideas for avoiding martyrdom are not new. However, just avoiding punishment for your contribution is hardly satisfactory. You want to benefit from your solutions. You want the glory and a share of the spoils. Some clever people want the credit so much that they would rather be martyred than lose it. So how does one have the idea, get the glory, and still avoid a figurative burning at the stake?

You may need to be selfish. Since it is dangerous to share a good idea, why not own its development? This strategy is really not as self-serving as it seems. Your martyrdom will not change minds. A successful implementation will force everyone to pay attention. Silicon Valley is crowded with successful refugees from big companies. Their employers weren't interested in breakthroughs worth billions.

Making your idea work requires the courage, persistence, and fortitude of an Einstein. But it can be done. You can do it. And there is great satisfaction in working for something that you believe in. You will never work harder than when making your own baby succeed. Forget about convincing the world—just use your idea to your own advantage.

You may want to rework your original problem definition so that your benefit is a key consideration. Start by identifying carrots and sticks that relate directly to you, even if you are addressing an organizational problem.

Carrots	
What good will come of a solution?	Peace Guilt-free prosperity A satisfying career helping others
Sticks	
What will happen if there is no solution?	War Epidemics Environmental disaster A dissatisfying, pointless career grubbing money

Figure 9.1: Carrots and Sticks

Then amend your problem statement to make your success a solution objective. It may be more selfish, but it will help you solve the problem.

Problem Definition: Create a successful, satisfying career eliminating barriers to prosperity!

BE GENEROUS

"A man will fight harder for his interests than for his rights."

—NAPOLEON BONAPARTE

You will be more successful benefiting from your great solution if many other people benefit from it too. You need their ideas and insights, so you need to give them a stake in your success. In 1982, IBM introduced the personal computer. By accident more than design, IBM allowed other companies to benefit handsomely from this innovation. A few years later, Apple introduced a much better personal computer that was years ahead of the competition. Millions enthusiastically adopted Apple's Macintosh. Everyone I knew wanted one, including me. But Apple decided that it should get most of the benefit of its innovation. It restricted others from profiting from the Macintosh. Only Apple could make or improve it. As a result, much more effort went into improving, growing, and expanding the IBM PC market. Trillions of dollars of wealth were created. Macintosh created wealth too, but much less for companies outside of Apple. There were fewer incentives to develop for Macintosh. As a result, its enormous technical lead disappeared. Macintosh has only a fraction of the market it could have had, and Apple only made a fraction of the money its innovation was worth, because Apple was unwilling to share.

Sharing the benefit of your idea is the best way to ensure that the best brainpower and effort are behind growing your idea. Shared ideas will be the most advantageous to you in the long run. So be generous.

Avoid Martyrdom

"To die for an idea is to place a pretty high price upon conjectures."

—Anatole France

The world needs solutions, not martyrs. As you use Einstein Thinking to create solutions, watch out for yourself too.

CHAPTER TEN

Einstein Thinking in Organizations

"Any intelligent fool can make things bigger, more complex, and more violent. It takes a touch of genius—and a lot of courage—to move in the opposite direction."

—ALBERT EINSTEIN

Organizations should be great places for innovative, creative thinking. They have people with varied experience and biases. They have the energy to grow even difficult concepts into phenomenal solutions. They should be hotbeds of creativity.

Sadly, the real world doesn't work that way. Most organizations are shackled by their own bureaucratic inertia. Simple changes are painfully difficult, breakthroughs are unbearable. As we discussed in the last chapter, creative problem solvers have learned that good ideas can be dangerous and are best selfishly pursued on the outside. This is not good for organizations or for the conceivers of ideas. Organizations need great thinking. Problem solvers need the power of organizations. It should be worth the effort to neutralize organizational barriers to nontraditional thinking.

This chapter is devoted to people with power over others who will conceive nontraditional solutions to problems. Innovative, Einstein-like thinking is messy and difficult, but if you don't foster it, the ideas and their rewards will go elsewhere.

MANAGING EINSTEIN THINKING

"It must be considered that there is nothing more difficult to carry out, nor more doubtful of success, nor more dangerous to handle, than to initiate a new order of things."

—NICCOLO MACHIAVELLI

Executives must make two changes to take full advantage of their organization's intellectual resources. They must learn to value employee ideas along with employee labor, and they must get over the waste and mistakes involved in creating superb new solutions.

Managing Creativity

"When the effective leader is finished with his work, the people say it happened naturally."

—LAO TSE

In the Industrial Revolution, management's function was to organize and direct the workers' hands to create a profitable output. This attitude is still prevalent in many organizations—managers think and their subordinates do. The boss was the boss because he had the ideas. Many managers still feel threatened if someone on their team has a good idea. The boss should be doing the thinking, not the subordinate. And managers feel outraged at the waste when a subordinate comes up with a bad idea. But in our post-industrial economy, an employee's creative ideas are her most vital product. Organizations cannot afford to waste the brainpower of their people. They need everyone's eyes, everyone's experience, and especially everyone's ideas to stay competitive and achieve their objectives.

Managing a creative environment is not easy. It is much more difficult to foster an environment of innovation and problem solving than it is to keep the assembly line moving. Managers whose people are not producing ideas are wasting their potential. But many managers would rather waste brainpower than admit that a subordinate had an idea they hadn't thought of. This is completely wrong.

Managers should be recognized for encouraging and supporting problem solving by their employees. A manager's job is to organize and direct the intellectual output of employees. When ideas are being conceived and developed, the manager is doing well. He or she should be promoted, not replaced by a creative subordinate. Managers should be asked about the creative contributions of their subordinates. What ideas have they had? How is the manager fostering problem solving? If managers are not evaluated on the ideas of their team, then most find it too easy to waste those ideas.

Get Over It

"There is no way to find the best design except to try
out as many designs as possible and discard the failures."

—FREEMAN DYSON

Breaking rules leads to mistakes and waste. There is no avoiding it. Growing ideas into successful solutions takes time and money, much of it spent learning what doesn't work. Organizations are not sympathetic to waste. They want solutions without mistakes. Executives must get over their concerns about the costs of problem solving. It is an investment that historically has paid off handsomely. A great new idea will probably be paying your organization's bills ten years from now. You must accept the necessary mistakes as critical to your success. Get over your concerns about waste. Mistakes are a vital overhead expense, just like you.

When organizations do try something new, they often make massive mistakes. They have so much bureaucratic inertia that only big changes get high-level approval. Mistakes don't have to be wildly expensive. Use small changes and limited trials to increase solution generation. You can make small mistakes faster. And limiting the scope of failures will make them more palatable.

Promoting Einstein Thinking

*"Don't tell people how to do things. Tell them what to
do and let them surprise you with their results."*

—George Patton

After management understands the need for subordinates to think
and is reconciled to a certain amount of waste, organizations need to do
three things to promote Einstein Thinking in the ranks. First, opposition
to status quo thinking must be sanctioned. Second, new thinking must
be encouraged. And third, heretics must be handled judiciously. These are
not tidy programs. They require an organization to deal with contradiction, absurdity, and confusion, just like Einstein did in creating his discoveries. But the rewards can be incalculable.

Question the Status Quo

*"Mediocre minds usually dismiss anything which
reaches beyond their own understanding."*

—Francois, Duc del la Rochefoucauld

Organizations must foster a culture that questions the status quo.
There is a dangerous human tendency, often called Group Think, to
ignore information that contradicts the current plan. People will go to
great lengths to hear exactly what they want to hear. Information that
doesn't fit is rejected.

Group Think is doubly dangerous. First, the popular idea may not be
the best idea. Closing your thinking to other information will not correct
that error. Better ideas are often obscured by popular rules.

Second, even the best ideas are imperfect. They share at least one sim-
ilarity to a kite, they both need resistance to soar. Opposition highlights
weaknesses and forces action to correct them. Albert Einstein was a perfect example of strengthening new ideas through resistance. Einstein
unintentionally made great contributions to quantum mechanics by
opposing it. He devised a number of thoughtful challenges that he

thought would invalidate the idea of uncertainty. Instead, as scientists found answers to his challenges, the whole theory was strengthened and advanced.

A healthy opposition will keep your deliberations honest. As good ideas are exposed to tough challenges, your thinking will grow and evolve to answer those challenges. Here are some techniques for encouraging opposition to traditional thinking.

Clearly Define and Communicate Key Organizational Problems

Clearly defining a problem is always the first step in creating a solution. This is especially important in an organization. Too often there is little agreement about what the key problems are. Everyone assumes they know and everyone's assumptions are different. Few organizations define and communicate desired solutions for their problems.

To foster Einstein Thinking, communicate the key problems in your organization. Keep the definitions at a high level to allow plenty of latitude for creative solutions. Make your problem definitions clear to everyone. You never know where a good idea will come from. If your problem was how to grow revenue by 15 percent annually, then "15 Percent Annual Revenue Growth" should be posted in every office. Anyone who is asked about the organization's key problem should respond, "15 percent revenue growth." Divisional and departmental objectives should be linked to this key objective. A customer service group may define its objective as "Reduce service call hold time to two minutes to support growing revenue by 15 percent."

Organizational problem definitions need their own carrots and sticks—the rewards for a problem successfully solved and the downside if it is not. Risks and rewards are not recognized as keenly by organization members unless they are in personal terms.

Create an Alternative Plan

Develop alternative plans to foster new thinking in your organization. The alternative plan should be based on a different set of assumptions from those used in your current thinking. If you believe prices will fall, assume the opposite. If you assume light competition, develop your alternative plan for heavy competition. Create options that account for these alternative assumptions. If you have already narrowed your choices to one, hold a brainstorming session to broaden your alternatives. Think broadly again with the information you have gathered pursuing your current course.

In the late nineteenth century, everyone was excited about electricity. Electric lights and motors were well on their way to revolutionizing society—except for one problem. It was difficult to transmit the electricity over a distance. Proponents of electricity like Thomas Edison had resigned themselves to putting a power station in every neighborhood to solve this problem. One would be near you today but for George Westinghouse.

Westinghouse had an alternative plan, or, more accurately, an alternating plan. He proposed using alternating current instead of traditional direct current. Alternating current voltages can be increased for efficient transport over long distances, and then decreased for safe home use. His plan was not well received at first. There were huge technical problems to AC electricity. And the public referred to AC as "electric death" because it used high voltages. AC electricity seemed dead on arrival.

But over time, Westinghouse was able to solve the problems of his less promising alternative plan. The problems of commercial DC electricity remained. It was Westinghouse's AC electricity that electrified the world. Today we all benefit from Westinghouse's alternative plan.

Don't rule out an alternative because it initially looks too difficult. Consider carefully how each objection can be overcome. It may be that no one has really tried to address key problems associated with the solution.

Lighten Up

Organizations can be grim places. Humor is an excellent resource for breaking the habit of old thinking. It was one of the key idea synthesis techniques we learned in pattern breaking. It is equally effective for deflecting scorn from infant ideas.

If you have an idea that violates important rules, introduce it to your organization as a joke. If someone else's infant idea is in danger of being cut to shreds, play with the idea to redirect its critics.

Humor can make even the most intolerable ideas palatable. In 1969, Eastern Airlines' Flight 7 was hijacked to Cuba, but the passengers didn't seem to mind when the pilot made the announcement. They thought it was all a big joke because Allen Funt of *Candid Camera* had been recognized as one of the passengers. Everyone laughed all the way to Havana, except for Funt, who knew it was no joke.

Freedom of Speech

Free speech is the primary emancipating political innovation, the idea that no one should be punished for expressing his opinion. It makes all other political improvements possible. And when freedom of speech disappears, so does political progress and innovation.

Free speech is equally essential to innovation and progress in an organization. When people are afraid to speak their minds, good ideas wither and bad actions go unchecked. To encourage Einstein Thinking in your organization, make certain no one is punished for speaking his mind.

Organizations also have a need for efficient communication. Time is money. No organization can provide unlimited opportunities for communicating divergent ideas. A good compromise that preserves free speech and efficient communication is to restrict the duration of communication, but never restrict its content. Set limits like one minute or half a page. Ideas that fit within the restriction must be heard, uncensored. And they must not be dismissed. Make freedom of speech a key element of your culture.

Remember the Value of Chris Concepts

New thinking should be encouraged not only because it may succeed, but also because even failed new ideas are useful. Chris Concepts provide the raw materials for ideas that do work. Pemberton's Pick-Me-Up was a failure as a medicine. But mixed with carbonated water it became Coca Cola and is worth billions. New thinking ensures a steady supply of both good solutions and their raw material—bad ideas. Never forget the value of Chris Concepts. Try putting a picture of Columbus in your conference room. Tell the real story of Columbus to your colleagues and remind them that even wrong ideas can be great solutions.

Devil's Advocate

Designate a devil's advocate to encourage questioning the status quo in more ordinary discussions. The devil's advocate's job is to challenge existing thinking. He is mandated with trying to break the rules when a group is solving a problem. A devil's advocate challenges procedures and regulations that are getting in the way, asking why they can't be ignored. He questions the assumptions behind a decision. He finds and tries to break the rules that are clouding the problem-solving process.

If a choice has a heavily favored alternative, a devil's advocate should ask people to switch sides. Assign the most vocal supporters of the favored solution to sincerely oppose it. This may not change their mind, but it will broaden it. As they defend the other alternative, they will be forced to really consider it, perhaps for the first time.

Shift the responsibility of devil's advocate periodically. It is a fun job and everyone can learn from it. It may also be useful to designate a more senior individual as your devil's advocate on critical issues. Otherwise, she may use her influence to diminish the devil's advocate's effectiveness. Everyone should be able to function as a devil's advocate from time to time. Just remind devil's advocates that they should encourage new thinking, not blast still undeveloped ideas.

Outside Opinion

Get an outside opinion. Remember that outsiders feel much less constrained to speak their minds. The outsider should feel confident that he won't be hurt in the future by speaking his mind, especially if it is his job.

Make it clear that you are looking for some fresh thinking, not a validation of insider conclusions.

Seek your outside opinion as far from your field as possible. If you had wanted a flying machine built in 1900, you probably would have hired an experienced balloonist. Balloonists were the experts on flying. But the best choice was a couple of bicycle mechanics outside the fraternity of flight.

Pay attention to more casual outside opinions. Listen carefully to what your friends, acquaintances, or rivals are saying about your problem. The rest of the world may be wrong, but listen to what they are saying anyway. They don't know what you know, but they are also untainted by your unique biases and will not be held back by your knowledge and expetise. Don't discount any input because of the source.

Hiring outsiders can help institutionalize innovative thinking. Hire people with skills different from the organization's core competency. A company of technologists could use some accounting-oriented thinking, while consumer products ideas wouldn't hurt an oil company. Outsiders are more sensitive to the stupid rules that trip up homogenous organizations. They should be listened to, and understood, even if what they say seems to make no sense. Outsiders should be valued for the ignorance that scores of industry experts cannot supply.

Support New Thinking

"It is a very grave mistake to think that the enjoyment of seeing and searching can be promoted by means of coercion and a sense of duty."

—ALBERT EINSTEIN

It is a tough world out there. Most ideas enter this world weak, undeveloped, and ready to be dismissed immediately. Ideas are like children. They must grow before they are viable. You must support the infant ideas in your organization until they have grown enough to be evaluated on their merits. Otherwise, your organization's best new thinking will either be stillborn or vanish out the door. Here are some techniques for preventing idea infanticide in your organization.

Listen

Innovators should be rewarded for their trouble with a hearing. Always be ready to give one minute to a new idea. Nothing encourages new thinking more than knowing it will be heard and considered. If you don't listen to wild ideas, people will never bring you their brilliant breakthroughs. So listen!

Let the creator know up front that they have one minute to state their idea so they can be succinct. Don't pass judgment on the idea on its first hearing. In the one minute it takes to relate his idea, the creator will think of at least one improvement to it. Ask the creator to think about it and give you another one-minute summary later. You may discard most of these ideas, and that is to be expected. But it only takes one brilliant idea to profoundly change your organization.

In addition to new ideas, your employees and colleagues have important observations and opinions that you need to draw out. Arrange to talk with each of them, one at a time. Make certain that you schedule enough time to draw out their honest opinions. Prepare some questions to get the conversation rolling, and let your guest know the topic in advance so that he is prepared as well. When you meet with him, just listen. Commit in advance that you will only ask questions. Don't make statements. Don't rebut. You will be tempted to defend your past actions, or to push for your own ideas. Don't! Listen and you will hear what you need to know.

Listening is an obvious way to increase new thinking about your organization's problems. But if it is so simple and obvious, why aren't you doing it more? When was the last time you listened to a subordinate tell you how the business could be improved?

Decentralize Idea Management

Einstein developed some of his best ideas while working in the patent office. As long as he did his regular work, no one cared how outlandish or revolutionary his physics ideas were. The development of new ideas should not be the exclusive domain of the functional group charged with related activities. That kind of logical organization only kills new ideas. Studies of creativity have shown political fragmentation and instability to be the most important external factor in spawning creativity. Societies that are chaotic are much more innovative than stable societies. New ideas do not survive when there are few idea czars. Great thinking emerges when no one can kill a new idea because it doesn't fit his or her agenda. Universities have traditionally been great sources of solutions. Problem solving at universities is highly decentralized. Colleagues work on conflicting solutions and no one complains about the waste.

To increase good ideas in your organization, decentralize authority to sponsor new ideas. Let people consider solutions that have nothing to do with their jobs. It is good for someone in manufacturing to think about a marketing idea. She is as likely to create a revolutionary marketing concept as someone in marketing, perhaps even more likely.

Decentralization increases the odds that a good idea will find shelter with a believing sponsor until it can grow to viability. Even smart people reject revolutionary ideas most of the time. Allowing employees and managers throughout the organization to embrace and champion new thinking outside of their responsibilities increases the odds that brilliant concepts will survive.

In an organization with real decentralization of ideas, everyone is free to pursue good ideas some of the time, even if just a few minutes each week. They can grow ideas that were not part of their group's charter. They will certainly waste some time reinventing the wheel or developing bad ideas. But the value they create in personal growth and great solutions will more than compensate.

New Idea Champions

Designate someone in your group to champion new ideas. Charge the idea champion with arguing on the side of new ideas as they are raised. This shields the champion from appearing ridiculous and losing credibility when new ideas flop. You will still discard most new ideas, but they will get a fair hearing. Every new idea need not survive, but they all must have a chance.

Ideally, a champion should be one of the more influential members of a group, like the boss. New ideas need strong defenders. Innovation thrives when the king sponsors new thinking. Martin Luther's revolution would have never happened without the strong support of local princes; never mind that their motivation was more economic than religious. Someone powerful should protect innovators from losing their heads.

An open mind is also vital. The idea champion should regularly remind himself that many of history's greatest ideas were dismissed as impractical, stupid, or ridiculous. Idea champions can also be devil's advocates, although idea champions need more clout to be successful.

Erect Protective Barriers

Foster new ideas by separating them from the traditional activities of the organization. Einstein had a tough time fitting in at universities until he became a science superstar and was allowed to do as he pleased. He created his greatest innovations when isolated from the opinions and criticisms of fellow researchers. You can give the same benefit to your innovators.

Use off-site sessions or idea sabbaticals to give the creators of an infant idea the opportunity to develop it before time pressures and traditional thinking crush it. If an idea shows promise, bring it back into the workplace with some additional physical protection. Allocate time and space for the participants to grow the concept to viability.

Sometimes just ignoring "skunk works" projects is enough to protect new thinking in your organization. If an innovator appropriates a few minutes here and there to work on an idea, let her. But be certain that new thinking is protected until it can stand on its own.

Resolving Conflicts

Einstein Thinking will never flourish if new ideas are consistently killed off by entrenched thinking when the two conflict. Even the best innovations can't stand up to ingrained rules. The first time concepts clash, the innovation ends up in the trash. New ideas must be given their chance to grow. When a new idea is in conflict with old thinking, try one of the following techniques to give the infant solution a fighting chance.

Common Ground: Look only for common ground, not differences. Both sides are too familiar with the points of contention. Have them work together to construct a list of everything that they agree on. Avoid more conflict. List an item only if both sides agree.

Add Players: New thinking is frequently rejected because it cannot find enough support in the immediate organization. Try adding players with needs and interests that allow the new and old solutions to coexist. A three-way deal often works where a bilateral compromise will not. To identify potential new partners, make a list of everything that each side brings to the table that the other party is not interested in. Make a second list of the things that are needed but not supplied. The two lists are a description of your ideal third partner.

Narrow Your Scope: If the conflict between old and new ideas seems too big to resolve, try to fix just a portion of it. List all of the issues involved, and pick from one to three points that could be isolated for independent resolution. Resolving part of your conflict will build momentum and trust to help with a more compete solution.

Start Over: Sometimes a conflict becomes too complex, the feelings too emotional, or the sides too inflexible for the current participants to find an answer. Try starting over with only the original problem stated in its simplest form. It will not be easy to discard all of the baggage that has accumulated, but if you can reduce your problem to one crisp sentence, you have a chance.

Handling Heretics Judiciously

"A man has no ears for that which experience has given him no access."
—FRIEDRICH NIETZSCHE

In any organization, innovative thinking will occur in direct proportion to the quality of the reception a bad idea receives. If a bad idea is rejected out of hand, there will be few new ideas. If a bad idea is considered fairly, people will innovate. And if bad ideas are recognized as valuable efforts, your organization will be flooded with new thinking. A few concepts will be priceless. Organizations must handle heretical thinking carefully to ensure a continuous stream of innovative ideas.

Einstein was probably not an easy man to manage. When it came to his science, he did what he wanted, or waited until he could do what he wished. Organizations cannot afford to do this with more than a few people. So it is important to create an environment that supports heretical genius without total organizational chaos. Below are ideas for keeping innovators happy while maintaining some order.

Recognize and Reward Bad Ideas

Recognize the courage of people who espouse novel solutions that either don't work or that you do not pursue. Radical, nontraditional ideas are not always good, but when they are, the benefits are enormous. Play the odds and encourage even bad ideas so that you don't miss out on the good ones. You could present a heretic with a symbolic "burned-at-the-stake" award. Acknowledge that he took a big chance in championing a novel idea, and that while you have decided not to pursue it, you would like to see more expansive thinking in the future. This strategy gives innovative thinkers the credit they crave and assures that they will break the rules again.

Preserve Rejected Ideas

You can't pursue all options, particularly if you are successful at generating many raw ideas. But even when an idea isn't pursued, preserve as much of it as possible. Chris Concepts are invaluable. When you can't pursue an idea, assign the idea's advocates to continue looking for opportunities where their idea could be tried again. They will be happy about that and encouraged to create again. If you need to discard an idea, write it on a three-by-five-inch card. Save the card. Encourage your creator by assuring him that his thinking wasn't completely wasted. You might want to keep a stack of discarded idea cards in your conference room to provide raw material for future ideas.

ENABLING EINSTEIN THINKING

"Nothing, not all the armies of the world, can stop an idea whose time has come."

—VICTOR HUGO

Regardless of whether you are breaking rules or just want to encourage good ideas, recognize the bias that always exists against new thinking in organizations. You must prevent idea infanticide and satisfy innovative thinkers even when their ideas cannot be fully pursued. You need solutions, not martyrs. Keep those creative minds working for you.

CHAPTER ELEVEN

Everyday Einstein Thinking

> "The important
> thing is not to stop
> questioning."
>
> —ALBERT EINSTEIN

EINSTEIN THINKING AND SMALL PROBLEMS

We have been using Einstein Thinking on tough problems that require much directed thought and iterations of work. But thinking like Einstein also works on smaller, everyday problems. The key to using Einstein Thinking on small problems is to quickly identify and break the rule that makes the problem so annoying. Try one of the four small problem techniques below. They are modeled on four rule-breaking techniques we learned earlier.

Do What You Want

You have an annoying problem. You probably aren't dealing with it the way you would like to because of some rule that you find inviolable. Violate that rule and do what you want!

During the battle of Copenhagen, Horatio Nelson ignored an order from his commander. When a withdrawal was signaled, Nelson put his telescope to his blind eye. Seeing no order, he proceeded to do what he wanted with great success. So however you justify it, do what you want!

Do Nothing

If you think you must solve an annoying small problem, then the opposite rule would be that you do nothing. Create a new rule that states "This problem will not be solved." That's it.

Scientific American once held a contest for the best explanation of Einstein's theory of relativity in three thousand words or less. Einstein reported, "I'm the only one in my circle of friends who is not entering. I don't know if I could do it." For Einstein, the whole problem of the contest just disappeared.

Delegate

The easiest way to solve a small problem is to delegate it to someone else. The problem is solved, but you don't bother with it. You have circumvented the rule.

Is there someone that should be helping you more than he is? Delegate the problem to him. Is there someone who would appreciate the challenge and responsibility of a problem that you don't find interesting? Delegate the problem to her. Or there may be someone else who also wants the problem solved. Offer to help him if he takes care of the problem. It's a good deal for both of you.

What Would _____ Do?

In the rule-breaking chapter, we went through an exercise where some highly competent person like James Bond was given our problem. The exercise was to develop a rule-breaking attitude, but it is also an excellent way to deal with small problems. Pick a person who handles problems very well as a role model. When you have an annoying little problem, just ask yourself what your role model would do. Give yourself special permission to act just like her. As you develop this attitude, you will find it an excellent way to solve small problems. Just don't shoot anyone.

Rule Breakers Beware

"Whatever you do will be insignificant, but it is very important that you do it."
—Mahatma Gandhi

You can't use Einstein Thinking and rule breaking to solve problems without some amount of risk. Einstein freely broke rules in his personal life that caused others much grief. Einstein did exactly what he wanted. He had a tough time recognizing limitations. If what he wanted to do was difficult, he did it anyway. If what he wanted to do was noble but dangerous, he did it anyway. If what he wanted to do was unfeeling, he did it. He simply didn't allow rules to get in his way. But rules like courtesy, consideration, and kindness should not be dispensed with lightly. They may be the more significant solutions.

Einstein Thinking Practice

"To be possessed of a vigorous mind is not enough;
the prime requisite is rightly to apply it."
—Rene Descartes

Einstein Thinking came naturally to Albert Einstein. He found that he had to shave very carefully because he was always having good ideas while shaving and often cut himself in the excitement. The rest of us can be just as creative. We just may need to work harder at it. Fortunately, there are some simple ways to build the Einstein Thinking habit. Practice, change, and tools can help you think like Einstein more easily and with greater effect.

Isaac Newton was once asked how he was able to make so many great discoveries. "By always thinking about them," he replied. It is good advice for all problem solvers. Like everything else, your ability to break the rules and get out of ruts improves with practice. The more you do so, the easier it will become. Incorporate one or more of the following simple exercises into your daily routine. Use them to practice thinking like Einstein.

Solved Problems

"Few are those who see with their own eyes and feel with their own hearts."

—ALBERT EINSTEIN

Resolving problems that already have a solution is excellent Einstein Thinking practice. Identify something that you do, like washing the car. Try to re-solve this common problem with Einstein Thinking. You might conclude that a regular rub with a dry chamois will give your car a superior finish, the underlying reason for washing your car. Thinking expansively, you may resolve that washing the car is a great solution for kids who claim to have nothing to do except watch television. You could even decide to move to Seattle, realizing that moving both satisfies a higher-level need and reduces the necessity of washing your car.

Use all the steps of Einstein Thinking to create a solution. Define the problem, generate new ideas, break the rules, and grow a solution. This exercise can be more than just practice. Problems are solved when there is a need. It may be that no one has thought seriously about this problem for a long time. There has been no need—the problem has a solution. But there is probably a vastly superior solution. You could find it. Just break the rules.

Stupid Questions

"Computers are useless. They only give you answers."

—PABLO PICASSO

Stupid questions are a great way to find rules that need breaking. Confucius noticed that many of his students were afraid to ask questions for fear of revealing their own ignorance. Confucius taught his students "Knowledge for knowledge, ignorance for ignorance, all is knowledge." Understanding one's own ignorance is also knowledge. If you don't know, ask. Only believing that you know enough is true ignorance.

To find more answers, ask more questions. Ask for clarification every time you don't understand. Ask stupid questions. Question everything. Probe and pry into the real reasons behind superficial explanations.

Stupid questions can be especially wise. They strike at the core of the unquestioned assumptions that may be the cause of the problem.

If you have an alarm on your wristwatch, set it to go off at the same time each day. Ask at least one stupid, probing question before your alarm goes off. The only truly stupid question is the one that is never asked.

Einstein Dice

"God does not play dice with the universe."

—ALBERT EINSTEIN

Regardless of whether God plays dice with the universe, the random throw of the dice can help you think more like Einstein. Dice are small, cheap, and easy to keep around. They are wonderfully random. When you think about a problem, roll a die and use the corresponding Einstein Thinking technique in Figure 11.1.

There are many ways to use dice to break out of a rule rut. Instead of pursuing your main option, think of six alternatives and make your selection using the roll of a die. Or, simply use the number you roll in your solution. Leave the dice on your desk to remind you to inject boldness into your thinking. Physically rolling the dice will prepare your mind to start breaking the rules. And it will help keep you out of a rule-breaking rut.

Dice Roll	Action
1	Improve the problem/solution definition
2	Suggest a trial solution, test, or experiment
3	Improve the motivation
4	Identify a rule
5	Break a pattern
6	Break a rule

Figure 11.1: Einstein Dice

Driving

"Curiosity has its own reason for existence."

—ALBERT EINSTEIN

Practice Einstein Thinking during your commute. Select a problem from your problem list to solve along the way. To spur innovative thinking, use the letters and numbers on the license plate of the car you are following in the solution to a problem. License plates are wonderful idea seeds, and you have time to think while you watch the road. If you need a clever theme for a trade show display and are following a car with an *L* in its license plate, then create solutions that start with *L*. Your display could have a distinguished Louvre museum theme with replica of the Mona Lisa, or use laughter to draw crowds. A laboratory motif could emphasize the science in your product or perhaps a Louisiana Cajun feast would get more attention. Use a license plate seed idea to break your old patterns of thinking.

CHANGE

"A fanatic is one who can't change his mind and won't change the subject."

—WINSTON CHURCHILL

Einstein Thinking becomes natural as you open your mind to alternatives. Change, any kind of change, can make you more comfortable with alternatives. If you don't like to change things, you are a prime candidate for using change to improve your problem solving.

Change your routine to open new patterns of thinking. Every element of your regular routine affects your patterns of thinking. Change forces you out of your rule ruts, making it easier to alter your thinking to solve a tough problem. If you usually start work at 7 A.M., come in at 9 A.M. when you have a difficult problem to solve. Use those extra two hours to exercise, read, or go out to breakfast. Avoid your usual routine. Then spend the last half hour before leaving for work generating ideas for solving the problem.

Reading Material

*"Any man who reads too much and uses his own
brain too little falls into lazy habits of thinking."*

—ALBERT EINSTEIN

People tend to select reading material that reinforces their rule ruts. Deliberately select some books and magazines that you would not normally read. Grab a sailing magazine. Scan a fashion magazine. Read a book on biology or Renaissance painting. Feed your brain a varied, well-balanced diet. Use reading to challenge your thinking. Consider new ways of viewing the world, like a skateboard-centric view. If you cannot tolerate a different point of view while scanning through a magazine, you will have a tough time considering a novel solution to a serious problem. Use your reading to build your Einstein Thinking abilities.

Leisure Change

"Science is a wonderful thing if one does not have to earn one's living at it."

—ALBERT EINSTEIN

Your leisure activities are easy places for more radical change. Changing your career, where you live, or your friends are serious alterations. But you can change your leisure activities this weekend. So why not mix things up? Find your favorite recreational activity in the list in Figure 11.2. The next time you would normally engage in that activity, substitute the activity preceding or following it on the list. Try something new. Give your brain a novel set of problems to solve. Meet some new people. Put yourself in a different environment. You can't help but grow a little.

Art

"If I were not a physicist, I would probably be a musician."

—ALBERT EINSTEIN

Art is a great way to improve your creative thinking. It can be the gym for your brain, building creative strength. Einstein was an avid violin player.

• Television	• Watching Sports	• Foreign Films	• Camping
• Water Skiing	• Shopping	• Complaining	• Raising Consciousness
• Skipping Rocks	• Mountain Biking	• Eating	• Checkers
• Comedy Clubs	• Espionage	• Working Late	• Reminiscing
• Golf	• Weightlifting	• Wine Tasting	• Running
• Hang-Gliding	• Basketball	• Reading	• Visiting the Opera
• Dining Out	• Rock Climbing	• Swimming	• Practical Jokes
• Ski Jumping	• Keeping a Journal	• Gambling	• Bird Watching
• Sculpting	• Kite Flying	• Mysteries	• Snow Skiing
• People-Watching	• Cooking	• Snorkeling	• Reading Paperbacks
• Singles Bars	• Stamp Collecting	• Sky Diving	• Sunbathing
• Sailing	• Sailboarding	• Softball	• Chamber Music
• Cancer Research	• Spelunking	• Bowling	• Surfing
• Diving	• Playing Monopoly	• Being Seen	• Naps
• Scuba Diving	• In-line skating	• Reading Magazines	• Canoeing
• Attending the Symphony	• Motorcycles	• Hiking	• Hot Air Ballooning
• Gardening	• Drawing	• Writing Fiction	• Bridge
• Auto Racing	• Chess	• Intimate Parties	• Squash
• Political Fundraising	• Organized Protests	• Fishing	• Talking on the Phone
• Racquetball	• Painting	• Dancing	• Visiting Historical Sites
• Cycling	• Movies	• Art Shows	• Drinking
• Stargazing	• Off-road Vehicles	• Massive Parties	• Plant Collecting
• Getting Rich	• Sand Castles	• Origami	• Collecting Autographs
• Horseback Riding	• Brass Rubbing	• Musical Instruments	
• Darts	• Tennis	• Home Improvement	
	• Rock Concerts		

Figure 11.2: Leisure Change

The violin provided a relaxing mental challenge with different rules and limits. There is no reason you shouldn't exercise your creativity through art, even if you think you have no talent.

A lack of skill is a good reason to avoid performing surgery, not creating art. Art is a wonderful way to unshackle your creativity. Create something new. Draw a picture. Write a song. Be bold. Be innovative. No one will die. Buildings won't collapse. Businesses won't fail. But you will build creative boldness in your thinking.

Career Change

"Work consists of whatever a body is obliged to do.
Play consists of whatever a body is not obligated to do."

—MARK TWAIN

A career change is more drastic than a change of leisure activities. However, many people have freed up their creativity by moving into a new field. Einstein changed careers from physicist to statesman and peace activist. The change presented him with an invigorating new set of challenges, and he rose to the occasion.

Mixing agriculture, engineering, science, politics, religion, and art produced some of our history's greatest minds like Jefferson and da Vinci. You increase your ability to break the rules by changing the focus of your career.

In our era of specialists, changing fields has unique challenges. We assume that one must have had years of training and experience in a field to make a contribution. In other words, one must be deeply in a rule rut. It is hard to contribute outside of your field. But it can be done. Nobel Laureate physicist Richard Feynman spent many of his summers doing research in biology, which was definitely not his area of expertise. However, the change of perspective helped Feynman to keep his mental edge by moving him out of old rule ruts.

You could provide yourself a similar intellectual vacation by spending a few hours working on the problems in another field. Find a clever person who does something very different from you. Have her explain the fundamental problem that she is facing. Understand the problem in detail. Then solve it. It will help shake up the patterns in your head. You may also want to share your solution with your friend. Even if you have a great idea, she will probably laugh at your naiveté. That isn't how things are done. Notice how her ruts are limiting her thinking.

If you are totally burned out in your current field of expertise, a change can lead to a creative explosion. Michelangelo's spectacular frescos in the Sistine Chapel are a good example. Michelangelo spent most of his career as a sculptor. Rather than being a handicap, his sculpting experience helped him create some of the world's greatest frescos.

The challenge of mastering a new field builds problem-solving ability. It is easier to recognize alternatives when you are familiar with the solution techniques of multiple fields.

THINKING TOOLS

"Give me where to stand, and I will move the earth."

—ARCHIMEDES

Archimedes boasted that if you gave him a lever long enough and a place to stand, that he could move the world. Today we have a great appreciation of the incredible "leverage" we can get from physical tools. There are few difficult physical tasks that we would attempt without powerful tools. But without hesitation we still attack tough mental problems empty-handed. Try using a tool such as a notebook or a tape recorder in finding solutions.

Capture Tools

"It is better to know some of the questions than all of the answers."

—JAMES THURBER

Thinking tools come in two different types. The first type captures ideas when you create them. One idea will spawn more ideas. When you lose an inspiration, you not only lose that idea, but also all of the ideas it could have created for you. Seize all of the concepts you create. If you can capture and use a few of the thoughts you have every day, they will lead to many more useful ideas.

Notebook

Many great thinkers have kept notebooks. Notebooks are perfect for capturing new, incomplete ideas. They provide a record of thinking that can be reviewed and added to. It is especially important to capture your outside-the-box thinking. Ideas that don't fit in your usual thought patterns can easily disappear because there is no context in which to fit them. They must be recorded if they are to be remembered.

If you find yourself in an idea slump, try going back through your notebook. Old Chris Concepts can serve as inspiration. Remembering previous good and bad ideas will open the paths into more creative areas of your brain.

Tape Recorder

It isn't always practical to write your ideas in a notebook. Carry a small tape recorder to capture your thoughts when you can't write. Tape recorders, particularly the small microcassette kind, make it easy to take notes while driving, in bed, or standing in line. These times when your mind is free to wander are fertile opportunities for creative thinking. Make the most of them by recording your ideas.

Ideas can be like Wordsworth's incomplete poem "Xanadu." Wordsworth awoke from a dream that he recorded as a poem. But before he could finish, he was interrupted. Later he could not remember the dream or how to end the poem, which is unfortunate because it is one of his best. You have probably had lots of good ideas that you have lost because you couldn't record them.

Even if you simply erase the tape later, you have strengthened your thought process by taking time to verbalize the idea. Use your tape to stimulate more ideas while you are driving. Just replay a tape of your thoughts. As you listen, the concepts you recorded will be strengthened and you will have new, complementary ideas as well.

A tape recorder is also useful for capturing all those mundane thoughts that tend to clutter our thinking. If you are constantly reminding yourself to pick up the dry cleaning, simply record a note to do it. Then return to focusing on your core problem.

Mental Images

You won't always have a tape recorder or notebook handy, so master one invaluable memory trick. Learn to create silly pictures in your head. Our minds have a remarkable ability to remember images. Even if you can't remember your brother's phone number, you can store enough images to choke a computer. When you have an idea that you cannot record, visualize it as a picture. If you think of two screws that you can eliminate from a product design, then picture yourself punting a couple of giant screws out the door while money washes over you from above. Make that picture memorable by enlarging key features to enormous proportions or by making the action ridiculous. You will find it easy to remember your idea until you can record it.

Creation Tools

"One dull pencil is worth two sharp minds."

—UNKNOWN

The second type of thinking tool helps you create ideas. They augment the mind's native problem-solving abilities by presenting concepts in a different way. Tools are powerful leverage for thinking like Einstein.

Blank Paper

Big, blank sheets of paper are magnets for ideas. When there is a place for them to go, ideas seem to pop out of thin air. Using a computer may give you a neater record, but great thinking isn't always neat. Blank paper inspires imaginative ideas. Have lots of blank paper around. Otherwise, the paper shortage may inhibit your idea output.

Colored Markers

Tough problems are not black and white. You should not think about them in black and white. Bright, bold colors bring out bright, bold ideas. Keep colored markers close at hand and use them when you are thinking.

Music

Music stimulates your brain's creative centers. Try playing a selected piece every time you work on your target problem. The music will help reconnect you to ideas you had the last time you worked on the problem. Here are some of my favorite selections for creative thinking:

▶ Pachelbel's Canon in D

▶ Bach's Brandenburg Concerto no. 2

▶ Ravel's "Daphnis and Chloe"

▶ Debussy's "Clair de Lune"

Non-Lists

When most people think about a problem, they make a list. To inspire new thinking, make a non-list instead. There are many types of non-lists. Draw a picture of the problem. If your local bank faces stiff competition from a large national bank, then draw your situation. Use caricatures or metaphors for the elements of the problem. Perhaps you would draw a huge monster rampaging through the streets of your city, tipping people from their homes. Or, you could draw a legion of zombies marching from the rival bank. Humorous pictures are particularly powerful vehicles for breaking out of your mental rut.

You could also create a map of the problem. Idea maps list the elements of a situation and connect them to show relationships. If you are creating an idea map for the problem of the local bank competing with the large national bank, then draw the flow of money in your town. Show the sources of big payrolls and deposits. Sketch where money goes from your bank and the rival bank. Adding the deserts, castles, mountains, and swamps of your problem will inspire even more creativity. Maps are a great use for blank paper and colored markers.

You may wish to draw the Einstein Thinking circles and plot where you are in the process of breaking patterns and breaking rules. Use arrows to connect steps and ideas. Be sure to identify and break those key rules.

Problem Boxes

Non-lists don't need to be on paper. You could put together a problem box. Collect objects relevant to your problem in a box. Handle the objects. Smell them. Listen to them rattle about. Even taste them. It will focus a different part of your brain on the problem.

Patterns

Looking at complex, visual patterns stimulates your right brain and can enhance creativity. Simply look at a complicated pattern or picture. Your brain will sort out the spatial relationships, and bring new sets of neural pathways on line to do it. These new pathways will then also work on your target problem.

Phone Lists

In Chapter Eight, "Growing a Solution," we discussed the importance of cerebral sex in developing mature solutions. Discussing a problem or solution with someone else really does help. Keep a phone list of friends that will discuss ideas with you. When you need a bit of creative inspiration, call one.

CONCLUSION

Our minds are marvels. They have nearly unlimited capacity to create and conceive. We may not all be Einsteins, but we are closer to genius than we think. Our unwillingness to allow our imaginations to run wild shackles our thinking. But with conscious effort we can come a bit closer to realizing our true potential. We can all think like Einstein, if we just remember to break the rules.

Einstein
Thinking Forms

"Not everything that
counts can be
counted, and not
everything that can
be counted counts."

—ALBERT EINSTEIN

During the Renaissance, traders in the Italian city-states expanded their operations into enormous trading empires. Making informed business decisions was not easy. Communication was poor. Transactions took months to complete. No one could accurately grasp the shifting trends that could lead to wealth or ruin.

A man named Leonardo Fibonnachi changed all of that. Fibonnachi had grown up in North Africa, where he learned double entry accounting from the Arabs. He took these methods to Renaissance Italy where they were widely adopted. With its system of journals, ledgers, and summaries, individual transactions could be rolled into insightful trends. Double entry accounting gave Renaissance businessmen a way to summarize their complex and far-flung dealings. With a concise historical summary, it was much easier to make informed decisions, and to make a fortune.

Fibonnachi's story teaches us at least two things. First, borrowing ideas works. And second, it helps to keep score. Einstein Thinking is also a far-flung process. Without some simple accounting to keep you on track, it is easy to slip into old habits of thinking.

Use these forms to keep your thinking productive as you break out of your ruts. They will help you define your problem, break old patterns of thinking, break the rules, and grow real solutions.

THE RIGHT PROBLEM

Problem List

List any problem that must be solved. Identifying a problem is often enough to inspire a solution. Recognize and act on the next step too. Most problems are not solved because of a lack of action rather than a lack of options.

Problem	Why It MUST Be Solved	Next Steps/Solutions

ENABLING PROBLEMS

Good problems lead to good solutions. Define the problem that you will use Einstein Thinking to solve.

Initial Problem Definition *Twenty-five words or less*	
Problem Hierarchy *Higher-level needs* *Is this the real problem?* *Sub-problems*	
Ignore Limitations *Is money limiting?* *Is someone's ego limiting?* *Is knowledge limiting?* *Is fear limiting?* *Is red tape limiting?* *Is skill limiting?* *Is schedule limiting?* *Is education or credentials limiting?* *Is commitment limiting?* *Is attitude limiting?*	
Ignore Old Answers *List, then ignore your current top three solutions.*	1. 2. 3.
Simplified *Define a simpler version of the problem.*	

You will need sufficient motivation to find a good solution. Create enough incentive that you will solve your problem.

Carrots *What good will come of a solution?*	
Sticks *What will happen if there is no solution?*	
Size *Shrink or expand the problem to encourage action.*	
Is the problem compelling?	

The Problem Definition

Define the problem that you will work to solve.

Problem Definition	

Idea List

Create as many ideas as you can. The more ideas you create, the more quality ideas you will have. Record all of your ideas for solutions, even bad ideas. Bad ideas, or Chris Concepts, can be useful too. They will serve as a catalyst for even more ideas.

Idea	Reasons Idea Will Work	Reasons Idea Won't Work

BREAKING PATTERNS

Seed Ideas

Use multiple seed ideas to expand your perception of the problem, and possible solutions.

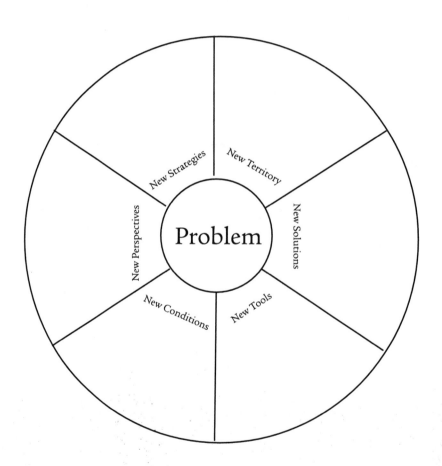

Idea Synthesis

Expand interesting concepts with idea synthesis techniques.

Humor *Use it in a joke.* *Create a humorous picture.* *Misuse the seed.*	
Visualize *See the problem.* *Point of view of seed idea* *Point of view of a child*	
Characteristics *Break it down into similarities and differences.* *How does it fit into its larger context?*	
Metaphors *Link the situation to the seed.* *What else is the seed like?*	
Applications *When could the seed be the solution?* *Change the problem to fit the seed solution.* *Modify the seed to be a solution.*	
Combine *Combine with old solutions.* *Combine with anti-solutions.* *Combine with another seed.*	

FINDING YOUR RULES

Return to the list of limitations you identified while defining your problem. Identify some of your rules for solving your problem. List those rules below. Use your ideas to identify your particular rules for solving the problem. Evaluate each idea and determine why it will or will not work. These reasons are also rules. Record them below.

Rules	Violate the Rule	Circumvent the Rule	Opposite Rule	Special Case

See what additional rules for solving your problem you can find in these areas.

Financial Constraints *Money needs*	
Lack of Knowledge *You don't know how*	
Physical Laws *Laws of nature that seem to be obstacles*	
Legal Constraints *Rules that could land you in jail*	
Custom & Preference *Unwritten rules or dispositions that are often given more heed than physical or legal laws*	

Review your list of rules. Break the rules that make a solution to your problem most difficult. If you are having trouble finding a way to break your rules, use one or all of the techniques listed below. Record your most promising ideas in the solution seed list in the next section.

Violate Rule *Break the rule deliberately and deal with the consequences.*	
Circumvent Rule *Eliminate the key circumstances that trigger the rule.*	
Opposite Rule *Create a new rule diametrically opposed to the original.*	
Special Case *Define convenient circumstances where bothersome rules don't apply.*	

SOLUTION SEEDS

Some of your most promising ideas may be seeds of a real solution.
Record them below.

Solution Seeds

GROWING A SOLUTION

Select one idea to develop into a real solution. Describe the target solution.

Target Solution

Ignore the inconvenient facts. Use rule-breaking techniques to get around them.

Inconvenient Facts	Violate the Rule	Circumvent the Rule	Opposite Rule	Special Case

Use cerebral sex to strengthen your thinking. Discuss your idea with many people, particularly people with different backgrounds and personalities. Record the ideas that they give you.

Collaborator	Incest Level	Ideas

You may benefit from a problem-solving partner. Identify your personality and skill strengths, as well as those you lack but need. Then find a partner whose strengths compliment yours.

	Skills	Personality
Have		
Need		

Try your solution in as many ways as possible. Push the boundaries of your knowledge by making mistakes. Record each trial and what you learned.

Experiment	Date	What Was Learned

Build your ability to take chances and break rules by trying something new every day.

Sunday	Monday	Tuesday	Wednesday	Thursday	Friday	Saturday

AVOIDING MARTYRDOM

Revolutionary ideas always generate resistance. Record your strategy for avoiding punishment for your solution.

Strategy for Avoiding Martyrdom

The whole purpose of Einstein Thinking is to free you from your rule rut. You can then identify and break the rules that are keeping you from a brilliant solution. You may wish to plot your efforts on the diagram below to help you see that you are making progress.

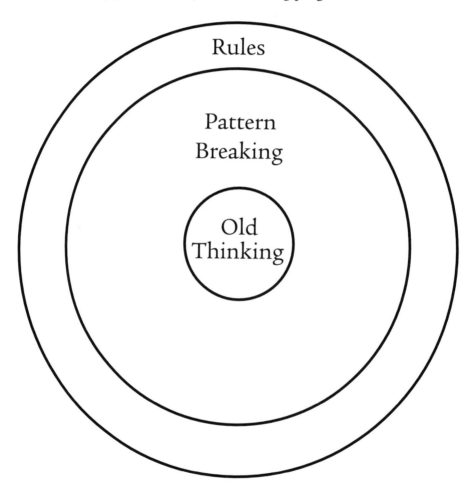

Einstein's Equation

> "Measured objectively, what a man can wrest from Truth by passionate striving is utterly infinitesimal."
>
> —ALBERT EINSTEIN

I have always been impressed with Einstein's equation for determining the relative time that elapses for objects that are moving at different velocities. I mentioned that I was surprised that I could understand and perform calculations that led to this remarkable breakthrough. However, I didn't include the calculations. One does not need to be able to do even simple math for Einstein Thinking. But here at the back of the book we will look at how Einstein came up with this remarkable idea:

$$t' = \frac{t}{\sqrt{1 - \frac{v^2}{c^2}}}$$

In 1887, when Einstein was about eight years old, A.A. Michelson and E.W. Morley performed a revolutionary experiment. They set out to measure the difference between the velocity of light as it propagated with the

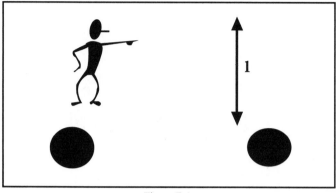

Figure B.1

motion of the earth, and the velocity of light as it propagated perpendicular to the motion of the earth. The idea was to prove the existence of ether. However, the physicists detected no difference. It drove everyone crazy. Here is why.

Imagine a beam of light that left a source and traveled a distance (l). To an observer traveling with the light beam, the speed of light and the time required for the light to travel the distance were given by two simple equations where c is the speed of light.

$$c = \frac{l}{t}$$

$$t = \frac{l}{c}$$

But when the light source was moved through space, there was a problem. Two observers, one traveling with the light source and another "stationary" observer would see light traverse paths of different lengths. If the frame of reference moved a distance d, then a second observer would see the light move a distance h. Since h and l are obviously different distances, the light must be traveling at different speeds for the math to work out. That is the way it works for rubber balls or sound waves.

$$h = ct'$$

$$d = vt'$$

$$l = ct$$

However, the Morley-Michelson experiment showed that the speed of light was the same to both observers. To Einstein's contemporaries, the

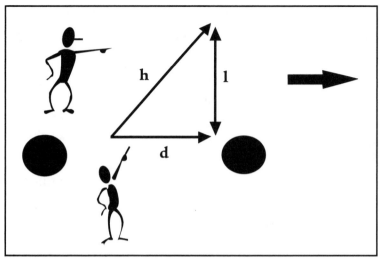

Figure B.2

experiment was a vexing failure. They spent years trying to solve the problem of why light appeared to always propagate at the same speed when common sense said it could not. They failed miserably.

Einstein set out to solve an entirely different problem. He decided to find what implications the Morley-Michelson experiment had for the universe. This was a great advantage because this problem had a solution. His contemporaries could never find ether or show that light was affected by the speed of its source. They would always fail.

Einstein began searching for his solution by playing with light. He imagined himself riding a beam of light. Practically, it was absurd to think of riding a beam of light. But it did get his mind out of the rut of the physical world of our experience. He imagined what he would see as he flashed across the universe. What would he observe about other beams of light? What would happen if he looked in a mirror while riding a beam of light? Would his image disappear? What were the implications if he could ride a beam of light and still see his reflection in a mirror?

Finally, Einstein broke a rule. He asked what would happen if the speed of light were in fact constant, but that it was time that varied. Fortunately, he had no experts to tell him it was a stupid idea. He simply redefined the distances the light traveled in terms of a constant speed of light.

$$h = ct'$$

$$d = vt'$$

$$l = ct$$

The v is the velocity of the moving frame. Pythagoras had already figured out what to do next twenty-four hundred years earlier. The relationship between the three lengths is simply:

$$h^2 = d^2 + l^2$$

If you substitute in the values for h, d and l, you get this equation.

$$(ct')^2 = (vt')^2 + (ct)^2$$

Next, you find a high school sophomore that gets good grades in algebra. Have her solve for t'. You don't have to do it all yourself, but you probably can.

$$t' = \frac{t}{\sqrt{1 - \frac{v^2}{c^2}}}$$

Einstein still had years of work ahead of him to grow this brilliant idea into the theory of relativity. But he ignored the skeptics, made many mistakes, shared ideas, and ultimately triumphed.

Index

About The Author

Scott Thorpe has worked in sales, marketing, design, and production in aerospace, robotics, semiconductors, computers, and medical devices. He is looking forward to his second IPO. When not trying a new way to make money, he enjoys skiing, mountain biking, and windsurfing.